The Mangyans of Mindoro

THE MANGYANS OF MINDORO

An Ethnohistory

Violeta B. Lopez

UNIVERSITY OF THE PHILIPPINES PRESS
QUEZON CITY, PHILIPPINES
1976

Copyright 1976 by Violeta B. Lopez

ISBN 0-8248-0472-4

Distributed outside the Philippines
by the University Press of Hawaii

Printed in the Philippines by the University of the Philippines Press

Alay sa isang pangarap—sa ikabubuo ng isang pambansang komunidad na kung saan maaaring mabuhay nang malaya't may dangal ang mga Mangyan tulad rin naman ng nakararami.

Foreword

THIS book marks the debut of a young author into the threshold of Philippine studies. Utilizing the diachronic and synchronic approaches, she presents enough data in a very readable and easily digestible style. The reader is provided a deeper insight into Mindoro's protohistory and history necessary for understanding the vicissitudes of life encountered by its aboriginal inhabitants.

Ms. Violeta B. Lopez's picture of Mangyan cultural history could be summarized as one of untrammeled independence during the protohistoric period, retrogressing into one of turmoil and vassalage during the Spanish regime, and developing into one of ambivalence and divisive policies introduced during the twentieth century under American rule. Ms. Lopez traces the origin of the policy of integration to the Commonwealth period, which policy was carried out with more verve and nerve during the early years of the Republic, but meeting with negligence thereafter, which sad state of affairs continues in spite of the Commission on National Integration (CNI) and the office of the Presidential Assistant on National Minorities (Panamin).

This book deserves reading if only for the knowledge of the problems persistently facing this and other minority peoples of the country, who remain the same slash-and-burn cultivators of old—illiterate and leaderless. The author proposes a policy of assimilation for the northern Mangyan groups with the Tagalog population. For the Buhid and Hanunoo groups, however, she thinks that "a more fitting approach would probably be one which recognizes their ethnic identity and even welcomes it as contribution to the rich variety of the Filipino national heritage."

The author, however, did not elaborate on how this aim can be achieved. Perhaps, a future study should go deeper into this vexing aspect of inter-ethnic relations.

E. ARSENIO MANUEL

University of the Philippines
Diliman, Quezon City

B	Early Sample of Mangyan Script	132
C	Author's Collection of Buhid "Urukay"	133

BIBLIOGRAPHY 135

INDEX 145

Sketch Maps

Mindoro at Contact Point with Spain	15
Mindoro as Charted in Fr. Pedro M. Velarde's Map	34
"Moro Pirate" Territories in Mindoro during the 18th and Early 19th Centuries	38
Distribution of the Mangyan Tribes in Mindoro in the 19th Century	46
Present Distribution of the Different Mangyan Tribes in Mindoro	68

Contents

FOREWORD		vii
INTRODUCTION		xi
ACKNOWLEDGMENTS		xvii

PART I   MINDORO FROM PREHISTORIC TIMES UP TO 1898

Chapter

	One	Pre-Hispanic Ethnic Continuum	10
	Two	The Mangyan-Christian Lowland Dichotomy	25

PART II   CONTACTS AND PRESSURES IN THE 20TH CENTURY

	Three	Perception and Reality in Mangyan Diversity	60
	Four	Pressures New and Old	83
	Five	Towards the Idea of Integration	106
	Six	Summary and Conclusion	121

APPENDICES

A	Sample of Hanunoo "Ambahan" or Songs	131

Introduction

THIS work is an attempt to view the Mangyan problem from a historical perspective. In particular, the writer seeks to delineate the diverse historical processes that moulded and shaped the present day problems of lowland-highland relations in Mindoro. This is a departure from the current trend in Mangyan studies which focuses mainly on these people for ethnographic or missionary purposes. The Mangyans have been viewed mainly from the anthropologist's and the missionary's eye. No study has been made to link the historic past of these people with the present problems that threaten their continued existence in the interior of Mindoro.

The island in which this cultural community may be found lies south of Luzon, separated from the province of Batangas by the Verde Island Passage. Mindoro is approximately 95 miles long and 50 miles wide, having a total area of about 3,794 sq. miles.[1] It is closest to Luzon, but in terms of its geographic features, some scholars consider it neither a part of Luzon nor of the Visayas. In fact, it is generally grouped with Palawan and its island clusters and identified as forming the islands of the Sunda shelf—the same land surface underlying Malaysia and Borneo during prehistoric times. Wernstedt and Spencer believe that Mindoro belongs more to

---

[1] Macario Z. Landicho, *The Mindoro Yearbook*, (Manila: Yearbook Publishers, 1952), p. 11.

Borneo than to the Philippines structurally, botanically, zoologically, and even ethnically.[2] Though the ethnic relation to Borneo seems rather tenuous except in a broad pan-Indo-Malaysian way, the close affiliations of the Mindoro flora with the natural vegetation of Palawan and Borneo, and the presence of abundant limestone material in many cliffs bordering the coasts of the island may indeed be taken as evidence for this theory.

The island's wide expanse of arable lands and coastal plains confined mainly to the northeastern, east and southwestern sections, and its proximity to Luzon and Visayas have continually attracted migrants from these regions. This fact is fundamental to the development of manifold pressures emanating since late Spanish times from the continuous influx of Tagalog, Bisayan and lately, Ilocano migrants.

Though a considerable number of studies have been made on the Mangyans of Mindoro, the writer realized at the very outset[3] that none had investigated the relations of this minority group to the greater mass of the Philippine national community. Hitherto, all existing literature on the Mangyans have been focused on their socio-cultural life. No attempt has been made to go beyond gathering anthropological data in order to provide insight into the problem of integrating this group into the mainstream of national life. All the same, before one could prescribe solutions to this age-old problem, it was necessary that there be awareness of the varying responses of this minority group to lowland pressures.

The writer, therefore, aimed at the outset to provide insight into the reactions of the Mangyans to lowland intrusion. But beyond recording the responses, the end-goal of the original plan was to provide alternative solutions to the question of integrating minorities into the national community.

In view of government activities designed to give the cultural communities greater participation in the moulding of the total Philippine society, it was thought that such an acculturative study would be highly relevant. For in the wake of changes, it is indeed easy to overlook the feedback of the recipients of all these measures, to assume all along that things are working out as envisioned.

---

[2] Frederick L. Wernstedt and J. E. Spencer, eds., *The Philippine Island World, a Physical, Cultural and Regional Geography* (Berkeley and Los Angeles: University of California Press, 1967), p. 428.
[3] Cf. Thesis proposal submitted to the Philippine Center for Advanced Studies on July 16, 1974.

INTRODUCTION

As originally conceived, the study was to account for the modes of integration-conflict in the relationship between the dominant and subordinate ethnic groups in the Philippine society. In particular, Iraya and the Hanunoo Mangyans were considered as possible subjects of study to show the interaction and reaction of northern minority groups to lowland penetration.

Two basic questions were to be examined, namely:

(a) What constitute lowland pressures to the Mangyans of Mindoro? and,
(b) How do Mangyans respond to lowland intrusion in their lives?

Rather than start with basic models for the study of minority-majority relations, the researcher aimed to come up first with a descriptive study of the minority responses before arriving at general propositions. In addition, a brief historical study of the Mangyans as a people was to be made plus an overview of the problems of majority-minority relations in the Philippines.

After an intensive study of practically all the available documentary materials on the Mangyans, the historical perspective of the research acquired more cogency, showing areas of understanding which could be meaningfully pursued with a view to examining in historical depth the subject matter at hand. The work, therefore, became basically historical in outlook. A significant number of ethnographic materials available to or gathered by the author herself would, in this sense, help in arriving at a more balanced picture of the processes involved.

This work is then based on a variety of historical materials from the pre-Spanish era to the present. Historical documents were used extensively to reconstruct the early forms of culture contact in Mindoro, as well as the beginnings of ethnic differentiation in the island. For the first part of the study, a survey is made of the existing prehispanic source materials, the voluminous collections of Spanish accounts of the colonization of the Philippines and other European works relative to the problem. The writer did not only rely on translated works. Whenever the original materials were available, these were counterchecked. In this regard, Dr. Zeus A. Salazar's assistance, particularly in the free translation of the various French and German sources, proved invaluable.

The second part of the work rests on an extensive review of the existing ethnographic data available for the period 1898-1975. It traces the ways "Mangyans" were viewed in different periods through the analysis of various ethnographic data stemming from the early "naturalistic" type of studies down to the more scientific ones of the present anthropological approaches to the study of traditional societies. Specifically, this section shows how the Mangyans became constituted first into "non-Christians" in the eyes of the external observers and then gradually, within this perceived ethnic community itself, into various differentiated groups. In addition, governmental policies are reviewed which constituted a pressure on Mangyan life from the American colonial regime to the present. For this purpose, extensive use is made of government records, ranging from annual government reports through the congressional records on policies and programs affecting the minorities.

Apart from the use of written records, the writer also undertook field studies. The first field work done in May 1974 was exploratory in nature—it was designed to familiarize the writer with her chosen area of study, and the probable areas for intensive research. Her actual exposure to representatives of Mangyan groups in northern Mindoro helped give definite form to the problem she had in mind. The second and final field work, made possible by a research grant received from the Philippine Social Science Council, proved very fruitful. Working on a list of historical sites drawn from the extant records relating to Mindoro, the writer came across a number of historic ruins which further confirmed inferences from the documentary materials used in the study. In fact, a number of artifacts were obtained, such as trade beads, Chinese potteries and porcelains which all point to the high level of the island's prehispanic culture.

Though the present study is not the first of its kind, it is clearly a departure from the current approach to ethnohistorical studies. While being ethnohistorical, it emphasizes the acculturative aspect of Mangyan history—particularly the responses of these people to various culture contact situations. Unlike the pioneering work of Felix M. Keesing, *The Ethnohistory of Northern Luzon*,[4] and that of William Henry Scott, *The Discovery of the Igorots*,[5] the present thesis goes beyond the simple study of the history of ethnic groups as they came into contact with Spain, or rather as Spain came into contact with them. It is definitely wider in scope as it presents a diachronic view of the Mangyan "problem" from the earliest forms of culture contacts to those of the

---

[4] (Stanford, California: Stanford University Press, 1962).
[5] (Quezon City: New Day Publishers, 1974).

present. In other words, it attempts to view the Mangyan phenomenon "from the inside," to the extent and the degree that this could be done through analysis of sources external to it.

This essay in ethnohistory is divided into two parts: Part I surveys the different points of culture contact from the prehistoric times up to 1898. Chapter One delineates the prehispanic ethnic continuum and shows among others that the Mangyan progenitors were among the first Filipinos to develop trade relations with the Asian world. Though the trade ties with China and other Asian countries were tenuous, this early form of culture contact was contributory to the development of a rich prehispanic culture in Mindoro. Chapter Two, on the other hand, deals at length with the diverse historical processes that shaped the Mangyan-lowland Christian dichotomy. It is further shown that the diverging native responses to colonial pressures—that of "withdrawal" on the one hand, and "submission" on the other—laid the base for future distinctions between "non-Christians" and "Filipinos" in Mindoro.

The combined religious, colonial and piratical pressures which are all concomitant with Spanish rule, brought an end to Mindoro's florescence. A further and more significant result was the intermingling and consequent "cross-ethnic" relations among the varied groups that withdrew into the interior. This "cross-ethnic" relations seem to have largely contributed to the growth of ethnic differentiation among the interior people. Moreover, the sources surveyed in this study allow the inference that the "Mangyans" may have constituted themselves as groups in response to outside pressures.

At the close of the 19th century, the term "Mangyan" was used collectively to denote a diverse set of peoples. The accounts written in this period provide a substantial picture of a people significantly different from the Hispanized lowland group. In the same period, the exploitative character of lowland Mangyan relations took form and was later intensified with the advent of American rule in the island of Mindoro.

Part II of the study reviews the different forms of culture contact and pressures which came with the establishment of the American colonial regime and the birth of the Philippine Republic. Chapter Three focuses on the perception and reality of Mangyan diversity as inferred from varied ethnographic materials published from 1899 to 1975. It is shown that while diverse Mangyan groupings had become known in the Spanish period, more intensive knowledge of these people was gathered during the American era and the years that followed. Thus, more ethnographic and linguistic areas were covered leading to a bettter ethnic differentiation of the Mangyans.

The last two chapters of the study deal with pressures old and new, including policy problems and directions. It is shown that in spite of the determination of ethnic divisions, the various Mangyan groups were still considered as a totality in relation to the dominant lowland Christian groups. Their relations to the Filipino community as a whole were determined and circumscribed in various ways. These policies ranged from "isolation" in the early part of the American rule through the modified concept of "admixture," and consequently, to that of "integration" under the Commonwealth and the Republic.

However, the road leading to Mangyan integration was fraught with obstacles. These obstacles took the form of pressures, both old and new. The old pressures were shown to have been institutionalized under the American colonial rule, and perpetuated even today. In our time, pressures on land, property and even life itself, comprise the new forces that encroach on Mangyan life.

Like many tribal groups in the throes of modernization, the Mangyans today face the threat of extinction. It is indeed ironic that they who have been able to preserve indigenous Filipino culture through centuries of foreign domination, should now give way to the compelling forces brought to bear on them by their own Westernized Filipino kins. Indeed, while we speak of "cultural communities" instead of "cultural minorities" in our day, the fact remains that the Mangyans and other traditional groups still live apart and away from their dominant lowland Christian brothers.

Acknowledgments

"Maraming Salamat."

What better words to use than this Filipino phrase to express my deepest feeling of gratitude to those who have made this study a reality.

"Kaya, maraming salamat kay Z."

In a special way, thanks is also due to:

The Philippine Social Science Council for providing the needed financial help to carry out this study;

Dr. Ruben Santos Cuyugan, chancellor, Philippine Center for Advanced Studies for taking time from his busy schedule to discuss the feasibility of the study and some problems in methodology;

Esteban Magannon, professor of Asian Studies and my former critic for his constant support and encouragement;

Mrs. Namnama P. Hidalgo, Charlie, and other members of the Filipiniana staff for making a number of vital materials and collections available for my use;

Miss Pearly Patacsil, librarian, U.P. College of Public Administration for providing assistance at times when I needed it;

Mr. Theo. and Mrs. Maria Herren, O.M.F. missionaries for extending warm fellowship, hospitality and for even making the necessary contacts with the Mangyans in the interior;

The staff of the Mangyan Bible School especially Hanni Kaspar, Mr. and Mrs. Andreas Farhni and Mr. and Mrs. Dave Fuller for being willing informants and providing accommodations among the Irayas;

May Johnston for lending me her manuscript on the history of the O.M.F. work in Mindoro, and Mr. Neville Cooper for making the necessary contacts among the different O.M.F. workers;

Atty. Ramon Moredo of the Christian Lawyers Fellowship for helping me locate the different historical sites, Pastor Gonzales for lending me his jeep and Atty. and Mrs. Gam Bongco for making some Mangyan records available;

Cora, Naty, Mrs. Ledesma, Rev. Toliver and Mommy for giving me the necessary encouragement and moral support; Jack, who out of sacrifice, typed some portions of this study and patiently drew the maps; and the Mangyans who willingly lent themselves as informants and guides.

Finally, praise and thanks to Him who made all things worked for good in this undertaking.

The Mangyans of Mindoro

PART I

MINDORO FROM PREHISTORIC TIMES UP TO 1898

For centuries, Mindoro exuded an air of mystery to all that passed through the island. The turbulent waters that surround it, which were of old the scene of numerous shipwrecks, the successive ranges of mountains, the diverse sets of peoples inhabiting the interior and the coasts, the exotic tropical plants and rare wild animals, the many rivers, lakes and streams all combine to generate a romantic aura.

Around this relatively unknown island grew fantastic myths about the "white race" and "tailed-people" of Mindoro. The 17th-century traveler-chronicler, Gemelli Careri, described them as a people with a "tail half a span long."[1] Le Gentil de la Galaisiere, a French scientist sent to do astronomical studies in the region, also made reference to the popular myth about the Mangyans at that period:

> It is said that in the island of Mindoro there is a case of men who have little tails, like those of monkeys. Several priests have witnessed this and have so assured me; and not long ago on the Pacific Coast near Baler, a woman was found who had a tail. Of this, I have been assured by the missionaries who saw her...[2]

Early in this century, a report circulated that Mindoro was the home of a white race with one woman; any man who had seen her never came back. The report originated in the imperfect knowledge of one American reporter who, translating wrongly from a Filipino newspaper, mistook a legend of the Batangan Mangyans for a real fact and consequently made of this group a purely white tribe.[3]

To this day, little is known about the inhabitants of interior Mindoro.[4] They are to the lowlanders generally known as "Mangyans," a term which upon closer study would not reveal much meaning

---

[1] "A Voyage to the Philippines" in *A Voyage Round the World* (Manila: Publication of the Filipiniana Book Guild, 1963), p. 133.

[2] *A Voyage to the Indian Seas* (Manila: Filipiniana Book Guild, 1964), p. 43.

[3] A. Henry Savage Landor, *The Gems of the East, Sixteen Thousand Miles of Research Travel Among Wild and Tame Tribes of Enchanting Islands* (New York and London: Harper and Brothers, 1904), p. 461.

[4] The Hanunoo, quite distinct from those groups living in the interior, have of course been the subject of a number of studies. Hardly accessible to outsiders, the interior tribal folks remain isolated today from lowlanders and researchers alike.

or distinction, except that of savage, mountaineer, pagan Negroes[5]—meanings reminiscent of a colonial past.

Yet, there is a sense in which Mangyans today still live in a colonial setting, unyoked from age-old exploitation of "outside peoples."

This part examines the various historical accounts which constitute an external view of the Mangyans and their culture up to the end of the Spanish rule. A history of the Mangyans as a people is attempted on the basis of the varied references made to them by Chinese, Spanish and other writers.

The origin of the native inhabitants of Mindoro can be traced back to prehistoric times. Though no organized archaeological exploration and research have been undertaken in the area of Mindoro, a number of materials have been discovered which lend support to the view that the Mangyan shares in the ancient past of the other Philippine groups. However, most of the existing archaeological materials were discovered by chance or through treasure hunting. This fact is true not only for Mindoro but for a majority of archaeological sites that have been located.[6]

Nonetheless, many truly archaeological finds from the Palaeolithic through the Porcelain Age have been discovered and analyzed by reputable scholars, beginning with H. Otley Beyer. These studies have of course set the history of the country to as early as 250,000 years ago. Alfredo Evangelista, assistant director of the Philippine National Museum, believes that if a deliberate search were made in Mindoro, the island would yield rich archaeological materials from as early as the Palaeolithic Age. As Mindoro is very close to the islands that

---

[5] Pardo de Tavera defines the term in *Etimologia de los nombres de razas de Filipinas* (Manila, 1901): "Thus in Tagalog, Bicol, and Visaya *manguian* signifies 'savage,' 'mountaineer,' 'pagan negroes.'" Blair and Robertson construe the word as applicable to a great number of people (Filipinos), but nevertheless specifically applied only to certain inhabitants of Mindoro: "In primitive times without doubt, the name was even then given to those of that island who today bear it, but its employment in three Filipino languages shows that the radical *ngian* had in all these languages a sense today forgotten..." Cf. Emma Blair and James A. Robertson, *The Philippine Islands 1493–1893*, Vol. 40 (Cleveland, Ohio: The A.H. Clark Co.) p. 41, footnote. Henceforth this work will be referred to as B & R.

[6] In the words of Wilhelm G. Solheim, the majority of the archaeological sites that have been located "were either found by chance in farming or building operations or through the exploration of caves. Most of these sites are burial sites. No reports on living sites, architectural sites, or stratified sites have been published" *The Archaeology of Central Philippines*, (Manila: Bureau of Printing, 1964) p. 1.

have yielded archaeological materials on the Palaeolithic Era, it is hard not to believe, according to him, that an organized search in Mindoro would likewise reveal the same materials.[7]

Of greater relevance to this study are the findings of Wilhelm G. Solheim on the Philippine Iron Age which focus on the distribution of pottery complexes in the southern part of the Philippines, including Mindoro. Solheim revised Beyer's hypothesis of the Philippine Iron Age which states that the Iron Age culture was brought into the country from the South by the Malays. In Solheim's view, iron was first introduced in the Philippines between 400 and 100 B.C. and was carried to separate areas by two or three groups of people:

> ...The "Kalanay" people, coming from Annam and Tonkin, settled in Visayan Islands, Mindoro, Marinduque, the Calamianes Islands, and Palawan. The "Novaliches" people, probably a trading people from some area far to the West, settled around Manila Bay and in northern Palawan and the Calamianes. Besides iron forging, these people brought with them the industries of cloth weaving and the manufacture of blue and green glass ornaments.[8]

Direct reference to the early Iron-Age site in Mindoro was made by Beyer in his outline review of Philippine archaeology. This site, according to him, was uncovered when a new road was being built from the beach to the town of Calapan. As reported by Beyer, the find "consisted of several interesting native pottery vessels, some strange looking gold ornaments, and other objects."[9]

Though no definite productive burial-sites were reported by Beyer in his 1947 review, recent chance finds have produced a significant number of porcelain, pottery and metal objects belonging to the Porcelain-Age culture. Chinese potteries and wares were obtained not only from amateur excavations but also from caves explored mainly by the Hanunoo Mangyans.[10] Beyer himself noted a number of celadon wares, mostly of Yuan or early Ming types which were obtained from

---

[7] Interview, April 23, 1975, Philippine National Museum.
[8] Solheim, *op. cit.*, p. 210.
[9] H. Otley Beyer, "Outline Review of Philippine Archaeology By Islands and Provinces," *The Philippine Journal of Science,* Vol. 77 (July-August, 1947), p. 260.
[10] The only other Mangyan group familiar with the use of Chinese potteries and porcelain ware are the Buhids. According to some Buhid informants, the porcelain ware which were handed down from their ancestors are used in offering food to the departed spirits.

"Mindoro natives, chiefly from the west coast."[11] In addition, he recorded Dr. Fletcher Gardner's exploration of some caves in Pocanin (1904-1905) where a considerable number of skeletal materials and jar fragments were taken.[12]

Until recently, however, the amount of archaeological materials found in Mindoro has been very minimal. For one thing the work of the National Museum has been concentrated in other islands where systematic diggings had been started. Partly on this account, the task of uncovering the rich historical materials buried there for centuries has been left mostly to treasure seekers and private collectors. At the height of such illegal hunts, wholesale pilfering and nocturnal excavations were not uncommon.

Notwithstanding this fact, excavations in Puerto Galera, Victoria and Naujan yielded many finds. In Puerto Galera alone, the excavations made in four grave sites found in barrios Bayanan, Minolo, Tangalan and Baclayan yielded "10,000 pieces (which) range in date from the 10th to the 15th centuries."[13] The immensity of such finds led Leandro and Cecilia Locsin, two of the leading Filipino ceramics collectors, to think that, in the history of Philippine excavations, the Puerto Galera grave site "is to this day unparalleled in the variety and wealth of ceramic recoveries."[14] This may be inferred from the following account of the diverse materials found in the graves:

> ...From the start of the excavations, Sawankhalok potteries of quality and infinite variety were encountered. Sukhotai pieces were also recovered although their number does not compare with the number of Sawankhalok potteries. Other recoveries consisted of occasional lead-glazed wares, spotted white wares, and early blue-and-white, a more substantial number of creamish white wares, gray-glazed wares, Ch'ing-pai, Sung celadons, Ming type, Ming Celadons, various types identified with 14th-to-15th century sites, an impressive number of gold and metal artifacts, large jars, earthenwares of a distinct variety, an endless variety of beads, and glass objects including bracelets and a few glass jarlets.[15]

[11] H. O. Beyer, *op. cit.*, p. 261.
[12] See also *Philippine Indic Studies* by Fletcher Gardner (Texas: The Witte Memorial Museum, 1943), pp. 2, 45, 48.
[13] Leandro and Cecilia Locsin, *Oriental Ceramics Discovered in the Philippines* (Rutland, Vermont and Tokyo, Japan: Charles E. Tuttle Co., 1967), p. 128.
[14] *Ibid.*, p. 128. The site in Bayanan where many of these materials had been unearthed has been purchased by the Locsins.
[15] *Ibid.*, p. 127.

In spite of such numerous finds, the excavations have no real value for research as there is no way of evaluating the recoveries except from an aesthetic point of view. Likewise, the sites had been so "disturbed" that an archaeological study at this point would be futile.

Apart from archaeological materials, a number of Chinese state documents, particularly in the Sung and Ming dynasties, further lend support to the historicity of the pre-Hispanic Mindoro culture. In truth, these written references parallel chronologically the Chinese porcelain finds in the Philippines.

Of greater interest to the present study are definite references to the island of Mindoro in the Chinese dynastic records. Chao Ju-Kua's important 13th-century account, Wang Ta-Yuan's work in 1349 and later Chinese chronicles all made references to the island of Mindoro. In fact while other local names cited in the Chinese accounts have never been satisfactorily identified, historians have been quite positive about the interpretation of the Chinese name for Mindoro. San-su, the only other meaningful Chinese term in Chao Ju-Kua's account that has been positively identified, has also been generally placed along the Mindoro-Borneo route.

Most of the details cited in the Chinese accounts can be found in the early Spanish records of the colonization of the Philippines. As early as the first contacts of the Mindoro natives with the Spaniards, records were kept by some of these "conquistadores." Written as early as 1572, these accounts speak distinctly of well-established native settlements which were not without knowledge of the outside world. For one thing, they speak of encounters with Chinese traders in the island of Mindoro. Evidence of the exchange of goods between the Chinese and the natives was manifest in the presence of native products found among the captured goods in the Chinese junks.

At this time, no marked distinctions existed among the Mindoro natives save for a vague reference to a group called "Chichimecos." This could have been the earlier inhabitants of Mindoro referred to in Chao Ju-Kua's account. Yet evidence is lacking to support the view of an ethnic differentiation by then. It is safer to conclude that what existed was a simple ethnic continuum, since no discernible form of ethnic distinction is reflected in the existing accounts.

The coming of the Spaniards brought about manifold changes in Mindoro, including the growth of a Mangyan-lowland Christian dichotomy. Pressed to move into the interior by the colonizing Spanish forces, the former coastal dwellers who chose to withdraw from the Spanish hold were cut-off from the overall pattern of Hispanization that took place in the island. This historic process later led to a marked distinction between the Hispanized lowland group along the coast and the inland pagan peoples.

The overall process of Christianization and Hispanization in central and northern Philippines inevitably posed a threat to the existing Islamic area force in the South. Stripped of their former territorial rights as well as restricted in many ways by the presence of the Spanish colonial power, a section of the Muslim populace responded by undertaking piratical assaults on the Christian settlements. Though piracy was a by-product of Spanish colonization, it also served as a tremendous pressure on the lives of the Mangyans caught in the midst of the Spanish-Muslim conflict. While this was taking place, the inland movement of coastal people avoiding the incursions of the pirates led to ethnic diversification which may have resulted from their intermarriage with the groups in the interior.

Thus at the close of the 19th century, we find the term "Mangyan" used collectively in early Spanish ethnographic accounts to denote a diverse set of peoples in the interior of Mindoro. Originally though, the inland folks may have been coastal residents driven into the interior by the coming of a more dominant group. These pioneer settlers in the island were the Negritoes, who are referred to in the early Spanish accounts as the "Chichimecos." The situation at the outset could have been that of Malay immigrants pushing the Negritoes into the interior, or to put in abstract terms, B displacing A by driving it inland. Yet while this may have been the case, the accounts also show that the members of group A were not totally cut off from group B. A minimum of social contact was maintained, primarily in terms of exchange of goods—that is, a bartering of forest products, which B in turn traded with foreign merchants. This may well have been the situation before the Spaniards came.

The coming of the Spaniards, who would constitute group C, brought radical changes in the status quo. In this case, group C dislodged B, B withdrew into the interior and consequently had close interaction with A. The product of such interaction is presumably the Buquiles, whom Jordana described as "a half-breed tribe belonging to the Negrito race," tan in complexion and not black. With C or the Spaniards in control of the coastal areas, contacts between B and the outside world (that is, with the Chinese traders and other Southeast Asians) could have stopped and free trade relations curtailed. This could have precipitated the spread of piracy in the region, and consequently brought in a counterforce to C, which eventually exerted pressure on groups A and B. However, because of C's advanced military and naval weapons, counter force D represented by the Muslim pirates, were overwhelmed and in the process were forced into the interior. These possibly were the Tirones (Tidunes) who contributed to the growing multiplicity of the inland people.

On the other hand, some of the members of group B who decided to remain in the coastal area underwent an entirely different historical course—their responses to C are reflected in a Hispanized culture which inevitably set them off from their kin in the interior. This historical process led to marked differentiation between lowland and mountain people. The influx of natives from other islands such as Luzon and the Visayas led further to diverse intermingling of lowland groups. Thus, at the close of the 19th century, the isolated groups in the interior evolved as the "minority group" in the island of Mindoro. Yet, while we speak of a "minority group," the problem of integration was not yet at hand, probably because in the 19th century, there was no concept of a totality into which they could be integrated except the Hispanized Philippine society. The problem of integration only becomes a reality when a total society either exists or is in the process of being constructed.

While we speak of social distance between Mangyans and Hispanized lowlanders, a minimum of social contact existed which was primarily exploitative in nature. It may seem strange, but the Mangyans were actually integrated into the worldwide capitalist system through various intermediaries among whom, close at hand, were the lowlanders and their Spanish colonial masters. In point of fact, the social relations among Mangyans and Christian lowlanders were laid down in the 19th century, developed during the American colonial regime, and perpetuated until the present time.

Chapter One

Pre-Hispanic
Ethnic Continuum

Hardly known to their progressive lowland kin, and living in the cultural backwaters of contemporary Philippine life, the Mangyans have generally been left out in the writing of Philippine history. Yet a thorough examination of the existing historical materials would show that they were among the first Filipinos to establish relations with the outside world. These early forms of culture contact are now here examined in conjunction with the beginnings of an ethnic continuum in the island of Mindoro, from the pre-Spanish era to the point of contact with Spain.

Pre-Spanish Mindoro

Though present day Mindoro hardly gives the impression of a flourishing trading port, it was one of the major islands regularly visited by Chinese traders long before the Spaniards stepped on Philippine soil. Early Chinese accounts of the Sino-Philippine cultural relations may be gleaned from Chao-Ju-Kua's work *Chu-Fan-Chi* (literally, *Reports on the South Seas Barbarians*) completed in 1225.[1] This gives us a relatively comprehensive account of the Philippines, especially Mindoro and the neighboring islands.

Chao Ju-Kua mentions the island of Ma-i, which historians today generally believe to be Mindoro. Recently, an analyst of pre-Hispanic

[1] Wang Teh-Ming, "Sino-Filipino Historico-Cultural Relations," *Philippine Social Sciences and Humanities Review*, Vol. 29 (September-November 1964).

historical sources wrote that "Mai is evidently Mindoro, for that island used to be called Mait, which is a southern Chinese pronunciation for the name."[2] He partly supports his view with the account of the Spanish friar Juan Francisco de San Antonio (Chronicas de N.S.P. Francisco en las Islas Filipinas, China y Japon, 1738) which, among other things, makes reference to Mindoro. Chapter 36 of the book is entitled "De la Provincia y Isla de Mait o Mindoro" and mentions Minolo,[3] the name of a settlement "from whence the Spaniards apply Mindoro to this whole island which in ancient times has been Mait." Mait, according to Fr. de San Antonio, is presumably a Chinese word meaning gold.

Scholars of the 19th century also referred to Mait as Mindoro. Notable among them was Ferdinand Blumentritt who gave to Mait the meaning of "the country of the black," which he believed was the name of Mindoro.[4] Early in the 20th century, Dr. Fletcher Gardner, a pioneer field researcher on the Mangyans, found the Hampangan natives calling the island Mayit. Lately, Scott records that the term Mayit is still used by Mindoro indigenes to refer to the region around the mouth of Mauhaw river, Bulalacao.[5] Olarte, on the other hand, avers that the fishermen of Aklan still call Mindoro "Mait." Of this controversial place, Chao Ju-Kua gave the following description:

> The country of Ma-i is north of Borneo. The natives live in large villages (literally) on the opposite banks of streams, and cover themselves with a cloth like a sheet or hide their bodies with loin-cloth.
>
> There are bronze images of unknown origin scattered about the tangled wilds. Few pirates reach shores.
>
> When trading ships enter the harbor, they stop in front of the official plaza, for the official plaza is that country's place for barter and trade. The local chieftain board the ship and proceed to make themselves right at home, and since they make a habit of using white umbrellas, the merchants must present them as gifts.
>
> The method of conducting business is for the savage traders to descend on the baskets and hampers all in mob, grab them and pick out the merchandise and then go off. If at first they can't tell who they are, gradually

---

[2] William Henry Scott, *Pre-Hispanic Source Material for the Study of Philippine History* (Manila: University of Sto. Tomas Press, 1968), p. 72.
[3] Significantly, a barrio in Puerto Galera where a great number of Chinese ceramics and potteries have been unearthed, still bear the name "Minolo." For a detailed discussion of historic finds, see *supra*, pp. 20-21.
[4] Quoted from Hirth-Rockhill's *Chu-Fan Chi*, as cited in Wang-Teh Ming, *op. cit.*, p. 405.
[5] W. H. Scott, *op. cit.*, p. 72, footnote.

they come to know those who remove the goods so in the end nothing is actually lost. The savage traders then take the goods around to the other islands for barter, and generally don't start coming back till September or October to repay the ship's merchants with what they have got. Indeed, there are some who do not come back even then, so ships trading with Ma-i are the last to reach home.[6]

While some of the trade items and information mentioned by Chao Ju-Kua can be checked against ethnographic and archaeological sources, whether Mai is indeed Mindoro, is not conclusive. There are scholars with differing opinions. Jose Rizal himself, after offering a geographical premise, declared that Ma-i should be in the Tagalog region of Luzon.[7] Wang Teh-Ming, cited earlier in this paper, agrees with Rizal and adds that "Ma-i or Ba-iac was primarily located in the Batangas region, including, besides this province, Cavite, Laguna and at least a part of Manila, Rizal and South Tayabas."[8] He gives reasons, historical, archaeological and etymological in nature, to back up his claim.[9]

Despite his denial that Mindoro is the land of Ma-i, Wang Teh-Ming does not discount the existence of trade relations between the Chinese and the early inhabitants of Mindoro. In particular, he considers Mindoro as the Min-to-lang referred to in Wang Ta-Yuan's account completed more than a century after Chao Ju-Kua. The reference to Min-to-lang which forms a part of the *Tao-i-Chih lio* or *A Short Account of the Islands Barbarians* is, according to Wang himself, a report of his two voyages in the South Seas probably from the port of Zaitun.[10] It is generally supposed to be the most complete record relating to the Philippines among the Chinese sources of the Yuan dynasty. Min-to-lang is described there as:

> ...important port along the sea coast. Owing to the stream overflowing the sea, the sea water is not salty. The soil of their cultivated fields is fertile. Rice and other crops are cheap. The climate is hot. To esteem thrift is popular. Both man and woman do their hair up in a knot, and wear black short-shirt, with blue short skirts around the lower part of the body.[11] They

[6] From William H. Scott and Ju I-hsiung's English translation in the *Historical Bulletin*, Vol. 11, No. 1 (March 1967), pp. 69-72.
[7] Rizal's letter to A. B. Meyer, cited in Wang Teh-Ming, op. cit., p. 405.
[8] *Ibid.*
[9] For extensive discussion of these points, see *Ibid.*
[10] *Ibid.*, p. 300.
[11] This closely parallels ethnographic accounts of Hanunoo men and women's clothing and hair fashion. The black short-shirt, long hair done up in a bun

dig wells for drinking water, boil sea water to make salt [12] and ferment treacle to make wine. There is a chieftain(s). Robbery or piracy is prohibited. When any one commits the crime, his whole household will be slain. The local products are: Wu-li wood, musk, sandal wood, kapok, and ox-deer-leather. In trading, the Chinese goods are: lacquered wares (porcelains), copper cauldron, Ja-Po (Java) cloth, red silk fabrics, blue cotton cloth... wine and so on.[13]

On the basis of the accounts cited, Wang Teh-Ming believes Min-to-lang to be Mindoro. He cites as proof the trade item "ox-deer-leather" which he interprets as one solid term—that is, leather derived from an "ox-deer"—like animal. He identifies this animal as the tamaraw, and sets this forth as a major reason for identifying Min-to-lang as Mindoro.

> Obviously, this animal is nothing but (the) tamaraw which "look somewhat like a deer and somewhat like a carabao." Hence, we may conclude that Min-to-lang is Mindoro. For Mindoro is the home of a fierce animal called tamaraw which is found in no other part of the world.[14]

Wang Teh-Ming further supports his view by pointing out that Min-to-lang is Min-To-Long in the Amoy dialect, and might well be Min-to-lo in old Chinese, "for as a rule, the final nasal of many Chinese words is a later development."[15]

During the Ming dynasty and shortly before the coming of the Spaniards, reference was made to Mang-Yan San and I-Ling in the Ming Annals, Tung-Si-Yang-Kao (*The Study on the Eastern and Western Oceans, 1618*). Wang Teh-Ming identifies these places as parts of Mindoro—Mang-Yan San as northwestern Mindoro and Iling as Ilin on the western end of the island. He added that "the people Mang-yan of the island may have the name after or for it (*sic*)."[16] Another term closely related to Mang-Yan San is Ka-Ma-Yan, a name

---

both by men and women were cited in Conklin's early work on this group. See H. Conklin, "Bamboo Literacy in Mindoro," *Pacific Discovery*, Vol. 2, No. 4 (July-August 1949), pp. 4-11.

[12] The Hanunoo Mangyans, a major supplier of salt to the other tribes living in the interior are known to make salt in this manner—*asin bilug*, the hard, rock-like salt is made by boiling and evaporating the sea water after it has passed through ashes. c.f. E. Iturralde, "The Religion of the Hanunoo Mangyans of Southern Mindoro: An Anthropological Approach to Mission Work," Ph.D. dissertation, (U.S.T., Manila: June 1973), p. 152.
[13] Taken from W. T. Ming's translation, *op. cit.*, p. 303.
[14] *Ibid.*
[15] *Ibid.*, p. 306.
[16] *Ibid.*, p. 413.

possibly transliterated from Ka-Mangyan, or the land of the Mangyan people.[17]

While it may not be absolutely certain that Mindoro is indeed Ma-i or Min-to-lang, it is quite clear from the accounts cited so far that the inhabitants of the island had trade relations with the outside world centuries before the Spaniards came and colonized the country. However, it should be pointed out that such trade relations were limited to the exchange of goods on the coastal areas. There is no indication of the existence of Chinese settlements or communities from the accounts—the prevailing picture appearing to be more of itinerant Chinese merchants trading items from one island to another. Therefore, no culture contact situation analogous to that of the present seems to have existed during the pre-Spanish period.

MINDORO AT CONTACT POINT WITH SPAIN

The idyllic trade relations between the Chinese merchants and the inhabitants of Mindoro were disrupted with the coming of the Spaniards in the 16th century.

Pressing northward from their base in Panay, the Spaniards first set foot in the island of Mindoro in April 1570. This drive northward was spurred by news of flourishing settlements and rich supplies of gold in the island of Luzon. Added to this compelling drive was the presence of Portuguese forces in Cebu which harassed the Spaniards to such an extent that Legaspi, the first Spanish governor-general of the island, transferred the settlement to Panay, "a place where no damage may be done, for never since these parts were discovered have the Portuguese resorted thither, and neither the king of Portugal nor his vassals had trade or commerce, nor can they possess anything there".[18] From this island therefore, the youthful and daring *conquistador,* Juan de Salcedo, was sent to explore the neighboring islands of Luzon, including Mindoro.

Salcedo's pioneer expedition is described vividly in an anonymous account presumably written by one of the Captain's soldiers. In the introduction to his account, the chronicler explains that he has ventured to write:

[17] *Ibid.*
[18] Andres de Mirandaola, "Letter to Felipe II," (Cebu, June 8, 1569). B & R, Vol. 3, p. 38.

PRE-HISPANIC ETHNIC CONTINUUM 15

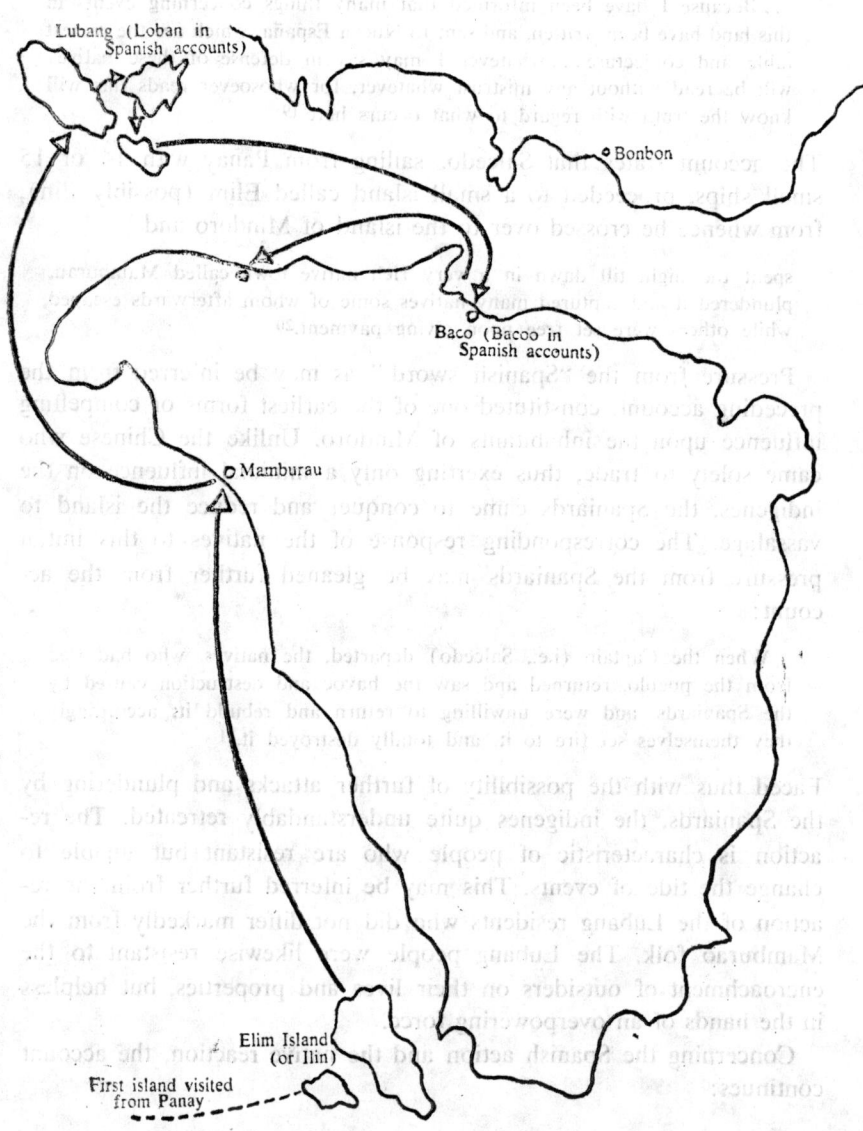

Mindoro at Contact Point with Spain: Shown in this map are the places visited by the first Spanish expedition sent to the island in 1572.

> ... Because I have been informed that many things concerning events in this land have been written, and sent to Nueva España, which are the merest fable and conjecture ... whatever I may say in defense of these natives will be read without any mistrust whatever, for whosoever reads this will know the truth with regard to what occurs here.[19]

The account states that Salcedo, sailing from Panay with 14 or 15 small ships, proceeded to a small island called Elim (possibly Ilin), from whence he crossed over to the island of Mindoro and

> spent the night till dawn in a very rich native town called Mamburau, plundered it and captured many natives some of whom afterwards escaped, while others were set free upon giving payment.[20]

Pressure from the "Spanish sword," as may be inferred from the preceding account, constituted one of the earliest forms of compelling influence upon the inhabitants of Mindoro. Unlike the Chinese who came solely to trade, thus exerting only a minimal influence on the indigenes, the Spaniards came to conquer and reduce the island to vassalage. The corresponding response of the natives to this initial pressure from the Spaniards may be gleaned further from the account:

> When the Captain (i.e., Salcedo) departed, the natives, who had fled from the pueblo, returned and saw the havoc and destruction caused by the Spaniards, and were unwilling to return and rebuild it; accordingly they themselves set fire to it, and totally destroyed it.[21]

Faced thus with the possibility of further attacks and plundering by the Spaniards, the indigenes quite understandably retreated. The reaction is characteristic of people who are resistant but unable to change the tide of events. This may be inferred further from the reaction of the Lubang residents who did not differ markedly from the Mamburao folk. The Lubang people were likewise resistant to the encroachment of outsiders on their lives and properties, but helpless in the hands of an overpowering force.

Concerning the Spanish action and the native reaction, the account continues:

---

[19] Manuscrito inedito, "Relacion de la Conquista de la Isla de Luzon," Fechado en Manila, el 20 de Abril de 1572, in Wenceslao E. Retana, *Archivo Del Bibliofico Filipino* (Madrid, 1898), p. 4. Portions cited were translated by Mrs. Consuelo Perez and compared with the translation in B & R. Vol. 3, pp. 141-72.
[20] *Ibid.*, p. 5.
[21] *Ibid.*

... The captain, having arrived at his destination at midnight, with all possible secrecy leaped ashore, and arranged his men and the Pintados Indians (Visayans) whom he had with him in an ambuscade near the village, in order to make the attack upon them at daybreak. However, the natives of the island, having been informed of the hostile incursions of the Spaniards, withdrew with their children and wives and all their belongings that they could take with them to three forts which they themselves had constructed. Now as the captain approached the villages at daybreak, and found them empty, he proceeded through a grove to the place where the first fort was situated; and having come in sight, negotiated with them, asking whether they desired to be friends of the Spaniards. The natives, confident of their strength, refused to listen, and began to discharge their culverins and a few arrows. The captain, seeing that they would not listen to reason, ordered them to be fired upon. The skirmish lasted in one place or the other about three hours, since the Spaniards could not assault or enter the fort because of the water surrounding it. But, as fortune would have it, the natives had left on the other side, a boat tied to the fort... two of our soldiers threw themselves into the water and swam across, protected by our arquebusiers from the enemy, who tried to prevent them. This boat having been brought to the side where the Spanish were, fifteen soldiers entered it and approached the rampart of the fort. As soon as these men began to mount the rampart, the Indians began to flee on the other side, by a passageway which they had made for that very purpose. It is true that thirty or forty Moros fought and resisted the entrance of the Spaniards; but when they saw that half of our people were already on the wall, and the rest in the act of mounting, they all turned their backs and fled...[22]

The existence of forts complete with moats reflects a relatively advanced culture.[23] Likewise, the writer's account of the weapons used by them in warfare underlines the people's knowledge of metallurgy:

Now since these were the first natives who we had found with forts and means of defense, I shall describe here the forts and weapons which they possessed. The two principal forts were square in form, with ten or twelve culverins on each side, some of them moderately large and others small. Each had a wall two estados high (lit., two men high), and was surrounded by a ditch, two and one-half brazas in depth, filled with water.

The small weapons used by these natives are badly tempered iron lances, which became blunt upon striking broad dagger, and arrows—which are

---

[22] *Ibid.*, p. 6. trans. based on B & R, Vol. 3, p. 144.
[23] The fort or "cota" still exists today and is located between Maliig and Lubang. According to Fr. Bernardo Pues, former priest in the island, it is about 80 meters wide and 40 meters long." cf. interview, April 3, 1975.

weapons of little value. Other lances are also used which are made out of fire-hardened palm-wood and are harder than the iron ones. There is an abundance of a certain very poisonous herb which they apply to their arrows. Such are the weapons which the natives of these islands possess and employ.[24]

Salcedo had another armed encounter with two groups of natives who likewise offered resistance, but while the first group ended up defeated, the natives in the second fort were able to hold their ground:

> On the following day we went with some four hundred friendly Indians to the fort; and the captain advancing within sight of it addressed them, asking they should be friends with the Spaniards and not try to fight with them, as that would result badly for them. They again declared that they did not desire this friendship and began to fire their culverins and discharge arrows; and in return the soldiers discharged, on all sides, their arquebuses. But during the whole day we were not able to enter the fort, for we Spaniards were very few in number; and the heat was intense, and we had not eaten, although it was near night. The captain, seeing that he had not accomplished anything, decided to return to the boat which he had left behind.[25]

The Spanish siege did not end with defeat for the natives, but an amicable treaty was reached with the Spaniards. As the anonymous chronicle recounts,

> ...the leaders came out of the fort and made peace with the captain, becoming good friends, which they are up to the present time. They gave him a hundred tall (taels) of gold which he divided among the soldiers.[26]

After this initial agreement, Salcedo returned to Panay with all his forces. He had, however, successfully laid the groundwork for future colonization of the islands of Mindoro and Lubang.

On May of the same year, the Spaniards returned to Mindoro with a larger force designed to finally reduce the island into a tributary of Spain. This second expedition was led by the Master-of-camp, Martin de Goiti, accompanied by several Spanish officers. Among them was Captain Juan de Salcedo. The expedition is recounted in an unsigned document dated May 1570. It is a simple but graphic narration of the campaign which resulted in the conquest of Luzon

---

[24] *Op. cit.*
[25] *Ibid.*, p. 145.
[26] *Ibid.*, p. 146.

and the foundation of Spanish settlements in Manila and Mindoro. Evidently written by a participant in the events, the account says that Martin de Goiti

> ...left the river of Panay with 90 arquebusiers and 20 sailors on board the following vessels: the junk "San Miguel," of about 50 tons' burden with three large pieces of artillery; the frigate "La Tortuga;" and fifteen praus manned by natives of Cebu and the island of Panay.[27]

After passing through the islands of Zibuyan and Banton, they reached Mindoro and anchored there with all the vessels in his charge.[28] The account speaks of Mindoro as the "lesser Luzon," not in the sense of it being inferior, but because of the unexpected presence of flourishing ports and maritime towns, "all inhabited by Moros." The writer also reports that in the "inland live naked people called Chichimecos."[29]

The description seems to point to the existence of two distinct sets of people—the coastal and the inland. While little is said of the "chichemecos" or inland folk, the coastal people are described extensively, especially in their reaction to the coming of the Spaniards in the island. The "Moros" residing in the river of Baco and the capital town of Mindoro are said to possess a large number of culverins, arrows, and other offensive weapons, and to have been entrenched in a very strong fort.[30] The town of Mindoro itself is described as an

> excellent though poorly-sheltered seaport. The harbor has only one entrance. Its waters beat against a hill which is the first and the smallest of a chain of three hills overlooking the port. The foot of the hill was fortified by a stone wall over fourteen feet thick.[31]

The people themselves are described briefly as "well-attired after their fashion, and wore showy head-dresses of many colors turned back over their heads." They are also shown to be in possession of large quantities of gold which they so wisely withheld from the Spaniards by deception, giving it "an outside appearance as natural and perfect, and so fine a ring, that unless it is melted they can deceive all men, even the best silver-smith."[32]

---

[27] Anonymous, "Relation of the Voyage to Luzon," (June 1570) in B & R, Vol. 3, *op. cit.*, p. 73.
[28] *Ibid.*, p. 74.
[29] *Ibid.*
[30] *Ibid.*, p. 77.
[31] *Ibid.*, p. 78.
[32] *Ibid.*, p. 81.

These same people are shown to be in close links with the "Moros of Luzon." Martin de Goiti himself sought information from them regarding the distance of Manila and the towns which could be found on the journey:

> ...While in this port of Mindoro the master-of-camp sought information concerning the distance to Manila and the towns which would be found on the journey. Our interpreter disagreed with the Moros of Mindoro as to the number of days it would take; but they all agreed that it was far, and that perhaps the weather would not permit us to sail thither. The natives of Mindoro added also that the Spaniards were crazy to go to Manila with so small a force, and that they pitied us. They recounted so many wonders of Manila that their tales seemed fabulous; they said that there were very large oared boats, each carrying three hundred rowers, beside the warriors; that the people were well armed and excellent bowmen; that the ships were well equipped with artillery, both large and small; and that any one of these vessels could attack two praus, and sink them when within range. With these accounts, the Moros tried to discourage the Spaniards; but the more they attempted to frighten them with such things the more desirous they all became to set foot in Manila.[33]

The encounter between the Spanish forces and the "Moros of Mindoro" is described as an aborted battle—the Spaniards more desirous of a "treaty for peace" than war, and the Moros divided in their determination to fight. In the words of the chronicler,

> There seemed to be a difference of opinion among the Moros, as was gathered from their demeanor, for some made gestures of war, and others of peace, some of them even going so far as to throw a few stones and level the culverins. On the whole, they were not very anxious to fight. Meanwhile the master-of-camp was so near them that they could have spit (sic) on him. All the Spaniards had already disembarked, and stood at an arquebuse-shot from the master-of-camp. The latter was so anxious to win over those Moros and gain their confidence.[34]

Owing to the peaceful attitude of the Spaniards, no battle took place. The natives wisely gauged the situation and took advantage of the peace-offering of the Spaniards. As the account emphasizes, the peaceful attitude of the Spaniards being quite evident to all, one of the "Moros"

> ...descended the hill, almost on all fours. Our Moro guide advanced toward him but on account of the great steepness of the hill, he had to be

[33] *Ibid.*
[34] *Ibid.*, p. 79.

PRE-HISPANIC ETHNIC CONTINUUM

helped up by the other Moro. After they had seen and recognized each other, and after the customary embrace and kiss, they descended to the master-of-camp. The latter told the Moro who had come down through the interpreter, that he need not fear, for he had not come to harm them. but to seek their friendship. The Moro carried the message to the others upon the hill, and a chief came down; and upon reaching the master-of-camp, said that he and all the town wished to be his friends, and to help the Spaniards with whatever they possessed. The master-of-camp answered that the proposition was acceptable; whereupon the Moro chief asked him to withdraw from that place—saying that, after they had withdrawn, he would come to treat of friendship and of what was to be given.[35]

Considering the strength of the Spanish forces which counted 116 men and 500-600 drafted natives, the response of the natives becomes more than just a case of passive resistance but a creative response to Spanish pressure. As may be gleaned from the following excerpt, the "Moros" did not fully yield at the first confrontation, but took every opportunity to carry out stratagems designed to give an outward form of acceptance while they bade their time for a mass withdrawal from the sphere of Spanish control:

> ...a Moro came with sixty gold taels, which he gave to the master-of-camp asking him not to get offended if the gift were not brought quickly, because the people had dispersed through fear, and therefore it could not be collected so soon; but he promised that they would raise the amount to four hundred taels. The master-of-camp received the gold, and had it placed in a small box, the key of which he gave to the Moro, telling him to keep it until the promise was fulfilled; but to consider that after treason nothing could be more blameworthy than falsehood. The Moro salaamed low, and said that he would not lie, and that *they would fulfill their promise little by little* (underscoring mine). And so they did, for on that same day, four more messengers came with gold; and all entreated and begged the master-of-camp not to be offended at the delay, if there should be any. With these flatteries and promises, the Moros detained us about five days, during which time we had friendly dealings and intercourse with them, although they mistrusted us to a certain extent...[36]

The delaying tactics of the natives gave them time to withdraw from the coastal town into the hills.

This is the first recorded response of import, for the process of withdrawal from the sphere of Spanish control later led to diversification of cultures among the natives who decided to remain in the

[35] *Ibid.*
[36] *Ibid.*, p. 80.

coastal areas on the one hand and those who decided to flee into the interior on the other. Without doubt, those who decided to remain within the pale of Spanish control embraced the Catholic faith and consequently absorbed Spanish cultural practices transplanted in the country.

THE CHINESE TRADERS IN MINDORO AT CONTACT POINT

An equally significant element in the same account is the reference to the presence of Chinese traders in the island, some of whom the Spaniards encountered in a skirmish at the Baco river. This corroborates the point made earlier in this study concerning the existence of trade relations between the Chinese and the natives of the island. For one thing, the trade items found by the Spaniards on board the Chinese junks paralleled those mentioned in the Chinese dynastic accounts. Thus, the report says that:

> The soldiers (i.e., Spanish) searched the cabins in which the Chinese kept their most valuable goods, and there they found silk, both woven and in skeins; gold thread, musk, gilded porcelain bowls, pieces of cotton cloth, gilded water-jugs, and other curious articles, although not in a large quantity, considering the size of the ships. The decks of both vessels were full of earthen jars and crockery; large porcelain vases, plates and bowls; and some fine porcelain jars, which they call sinoratas. They also found iron, copper, steel, and a small quantity of bees wax which the Chinese had bought.[37]

The writer adds that the Chinese were known to the natives as *sangleyes*, which meant nothing more than "travelling merchants." The Spaniards found several *sangleyes* in Mindoro, some in a skirmish at the Baco river area. While the original intent of Martin de Goiti was to "request peace and friendship with them," the Spaniard arquebusiers who reached the river ahead of the master-of-camp, engaged the Chinese in a short battle which ended in the death of 20 Chinese traders:

> ...At the break of day, the praus which had preceded the others reached the river where the Chinese ships were anchored. The Chinese, either because news of the Spaniards had reached them, or because they had heard arquebuse shots, were coming out side by side with foresails up, beating on drums, playing on fifes, firing rockets and culverins, and making a great

[37] *Ibid.*, p. 76.

warlike display. Many of them were seen on deck, armed with arquebuses and unsheathed cutlasses. The Spaniards, who are not at all slothful, did not refuse the challenge offered them by the Chinese; on the contrary, they bodily and fearlessly attacked the Chinese ships and, with their usual courage grappled with them... the goodly aim of the arquebusiers was so effective that the Chinese did not leave their shelter, and the Spaniards were thus enabled to board their ship and take possession of them.[38]

Martin de Goiti "showed much displeasure when he heard of the occurrence." To make up for the breach of maritime courtesy, he set the Chinese free and provided assistance for the repair of their ship. This gesture was "highly appreciated by the Chinese who, being very humble people, knelt down with loud utterances of joy."[39]

At point of contact with Spain, therefore, Mindoro was an island of relative importance. It was frequently visited not only by native traders from other Philippine islands such as Luzon and further south in the Visayas, but also foreign traders like the traveling Chinese merchants. The coastal people whom the Spaniards encountered were thus not without experience in dealing with aliens and itinerant travelers. It is likely that the island even served as a commercial port where not only Chinese but other Southeast Asian nationalities as well loaded and unloaded their goods. The "town of Mindoro" (as described in the Spanish account) appears in fact to have been an excellent seaport—an asset which the Spaniards did not leave untapped for shortly after colonizing the island, they turned it into a major port-of-call for vessels coming from New Spain and the islands of the "Pintados." Thus, one should not speak of Spain's discovery of the island nor any other part of the Philippines; the Spanish accounts of the state-of-affairs at the time they came into the archipelago discount the whole idea. At any rate, the Spanish historians themselves speak of maritime towns or pueblos, of fortified forts and moats, even a "stone wall over 14 feet thick in the island of Mindoro."

The coastal people are described as having a relatively advanced culture, with a diverse collection of arms and elaborate forms of defense against possible intruders. They are also known as fancy dressers and owners of large quantities of gold. As the Spanish writers themselves recognized, the inhabitants were not only skilled warriors

[38] *Ibid.*, p. 75.
[39] *Ibid.*, p. 76.

but also a resilient people—innovative even in the face of defeat. Furthermore, the Spaniards encountered in the island a semblance of organized religion which, ironically, had posed the same challenge to Christianity in their own homeland. This was Islam.

In all likelihood, the "Moros of Mindoro," as they are described in the Spanish accounts, were proselytes of the roaming Bornean preacher-traders that undertook Islamic missionary activities in different parts of the country shortly before the Spaniards came. It is also possible that some Borneans themselves formed settlements among the older inhabitants of the coastal areas of Mindoro and exercised some form of authority among the indigenes of the island.[40] Nonetheless, the accounts do not verify the existence of deeply embedded Islamic practices, save one reference in a letter of Fray de Albuquerque which mentions among other things that "some inhabitants in Mindoro killed pigs out of sheer hatred for them, whereas they killed goats with special ceremonies." The people described may well be the Muslim Bornean settlers among the native inhabitants of Mindoro.

Around this period, too, ethnic distinctions among inland coastal peoples were already noted in the Spanish accounts. These were, however, still vague for the Spanish expeditions did not go beyond the coastal areas. The "Chichimecos" or inland folks may well be the pioneer settlers, driven into the interior by the arrival and immigration of Borneans in the island. With the coming of the Spaniards, a new movement into the interior would be observed, causing a shift in the geographic distribution of the inhabitants of the island. This time the "push factor" would be the Spanish colonizers bent on reducing the natives into vassals and tributaries of Spain.

---

[40] Prof. Cesar A. Majul attests to the existence of Bornean settlements in Manila and construes that some of the rulers found by the Spaniards were themselves Borneans. He in fact cites that as late as 1574, the Borneans and their allies, the Sulus, continued to extract tribute from the natives of Mindoro, thus this practice must have been going on for quite some time. Cf. *Muslims in the Philippines* (Quezon City: University of the Philippines Press, 1973), pp. 72-78.

CHAPTER TWO

The Mangyan-Christian
Lowland Dichotomy

IF in the previous period there appears a tenuous distinction between "inland" and "coastal" groups in Mindoro—i.e., an undefined differentiation between inland and coastal peoples, in the succeeding period (from 1570 to the end of the 19th century), a new distinction would become evident. A product of the long process of Hispanization, this distinction would be mainly that between Christian-lowland and highland or interior groups. As a result of missionary activity and greater exposure of both Spaniards and foreigners alike to the natives of the island, there would ensue a better knowledge of the Mangyans, making this "Mangyan-Christian dichotomy" break down a little towards the end of the Spanish rule.

RELIGIOUS PRESSURE AND EARLY MANGYAN RESPONSE

Religious evangelization in Mindoro and with it, the compelling influence of the friars, started alongside the pacification of the island in 1570. Colin observes that side by side with Salcedo's soldiers came preachers of the Faith, who went to the island to convert the natives.[1] In 1575, a letter to Phillip II from a Spanish captain named Juan Pacheco Maldonado reports, among other things, the presence of the Augustinian order in Mindoro. Mindoro is included in the list

[1] Francisco Colin, S.J. *Labor Evangelica* (Madrid, 1663) rep. in 3 vol. ed. Pablo Pastell, Barcelona, 1900-1902, Vol. 1, p. 132.

of five places where religious monasteries could be found in the country and is considered one of the relatively few areas "where a great number of Indians have been converted."[2]

Contrary to what one writer believes,[3] the pioneer religious workers in Mindoro were the Augustinian missionaries and not the Jesuits. Among those pioneer Augustinian preachers were Diego Mojica and Francisco de Ortega. Mojica was sent to the island in 1573, and Ortega was reassigned and appointed prior of the convent of Manila in 1575, after a near-death encounter in the hands of the "Moros of Mindoro."[4] Juan de Medina throws light on this event which was occasioned by Limahong's attack on Manila, whence the pirates spread rumors that the Spaniards had all been killed. Medina records that those "who hastened to believe" the rumors

> ...were the Indians of Mindoro, who are also something like the Moros... As soon as those Moros heard, then, of the result at Manila, they threw off the yoke, attacked the fathers, seized them, and talked of killing them. However, they forbode to kill the fathers immediately I know not for what reasons since the Moros were setting out to execute that resolve.[5]

At the start, the influence of the missionaries did not go beyond the village of Baco, where only one minister labored for years. At that time the flourishing coastal villages noted in the early Spanish accounts had all but disappeared, as may be gleaned from Ortega's report which came out in 1594. In it, Mindoro appears

> ...but scantily populated. Although much of it has not been visited, in the known parts there are about 2000 Indian tributarios. The chief village of the island (which belongs to your Highness), has one minister. There is need of 6 ministers of the one priest that it has.[6]

---

[2] Juan Pacheco Maldonado, "Letter to Felipe II, Manila (1575?)," in B & R, Vol. 3, 1569-1576, p. 299.

[3] Macario Z. Landicho, "Ecclesiastical Administration" in *Mindoro Yearbook* (Manila: Year Book Publishers, 1952), p. 126.

[4] Juan de Medina O. S. A., *History of the Augustinian Order in the Filipinas Islands*, 1630, in B & R, Vol. 22, 1629-1630, p. 222.

[5] *Ibid.*

[6] Fray Francisco de Ortega, "Report Concerning the Filipinas Islands and Other Papers," in B & R, Vol. 8, p. 98. Wang Teh Ming likewise notes that during the Ming dynasty, references to Ma-i, (the most important place in the Philippines mentioned in earlier Chinese accounts), had disappeared as "Lu-song" emerged in the Ming accounts. cf. Wang Teh-Ming, "Sino-Filipino Historico-Cultural Relations," *Philippine Social Sciences and Humanities Review*, Vol. 29 (September-November 1964), p. 307.

The scarcity of religious workers in Mindoro may have led to the assignment of the seculars in the area. Yet, this move apparently did not change the general lag in religious evangelization. In 1626, the secular priest of Naujan, which appears to be the principal town of Mindoro at this time, sought the help of a Jesuit, Domingo de Peñalver. The Jesuit's mission was to win the people of the thickly forested interior, the "Mangians," about whose conversion nothing had as yet been done. Peñalver's successful two-month mission gave the diocesan clergy of Mindoro the idea of asking the Jesuits to establish themselves permanently in the island for the purpose of evangelizing the interior inhabitants while they took care of the settled and prospering Tagalog towns along the coasts. This plan was carried out in 1631. That year, Mindoro and Marinduque were merged into a single mission, with three priests in residence at Naujan and two in Marinduque.[7] A preliminary survey made by the zealous Jesuit workers placed the interior population at 6,000.

An interesting point to note at this period is the already-evolving pattern of distinction set between the coastal and interior natives especially in terms of ecclesiastical administration. The accounts speak of Tagalogs settling on the seacoast, and it may well be that they were converts who formed *reducciones,* or agglomerated settlements — they were proselytes of the new religion which called for their allegiance to the Spanish cross and crown.

One of the earliest references to the "Mangyans" was made by Fray Medina who identified them as "other Indians, whiter than the Tagals, living in troops in the mountains."[8] Except for the apparent difference in color which, obviously, was more a consequence of the Tagals' greater exposure to the sun in the coastal areas, no other marked differences were recorded.

Medina describes the Mangyans as:

> ... the ancient inhabitants of the country, and it is they who gather the great abundance of wax which is yielded there ... They are very good, and if they were instructed and taught, it would be easy to reduce them to settlements and missions.[9]

---

[7] From the Annual Letter of the Jesuit Philippine Province for 1632, a manuscript preserved in the Roman Archives of the Society of Jesus, cited in H. de la Costa, S.J. *Readings in Philippine History* (Manila: 1965, 1973), pp. 1-2.
[8] Medina, *op. cit.,* p. 223.
[9] *Ibid.*

It is possible that these same people described by Medina were the "Chichemecos" reported in the account of Martin de Goiti's expedition to the island. From Medina's account it is quite clear that the Mangyans themselves were inland peoples. The good friar remarks that "these Mangyans" especially

> ...fear the sea. They pay no tribute. They fear lest the Spaniards take them to man their ships. They go naked; and deliver the wax to the Tagals, which the latter pay as tribute, and give as their share. More than three hundred quintals of wax yearly must be obtained in this island.[10]

A chain of exploitation is evident from the account—that is, lowlanders exploited the Mangyans and the lowlanders were in turn exploited by the Spaniards. Direct interaction between these mountain peoples and the Spaniards was well nigh impossible in view of the nomadic life of the former. Consequently, direct missionary effort to reach the Mangyans began only in 1631, more than half a century after the Spaniards set foot in the island.

Velarde's account of the Mangyans does not differ markedly from Medina's description of them. He likewise describes them as a nomadic people, with no fixed habitation and living only on wild fruits and root crops. Obviously, the descriptions do not fit the coastal people found by Salcedo and the pioneer Spanish explorers in the islands. More extensively, Velarde reports that

> ...These people wandered through the mountains and woods there like the wild deer, and went about entirely naked, wearing only a breech-cloth (bahaque) for the sake of decency; they had no house, hearth, or fixed habitation; and they slept where night overtook them, in a cave or in the trunk of some tree(s). They gathered their food on the trees or in the fields, since it was reduced to wild fruits and roots; and as their greatest treat they ate rice boiled in water. Their furnishings were some bows and arrows, or javelins for hunting and a jar for cooking rice, and he who secured a knife or an iron instrument, thought they had a Potosi (?). They acknowledged no deity, and when they had any good fortune the entire barangay (or family connection) killed and ate carabao or buffalo; and what was left they sacrificed to the souls of their ancestors.[11]

---

[10] *Ibid., loc. cit.*
[11] Pedro Murillo Velarde, *Historia de la Provincia De Philippinas de la Compania De Jesus,* Segunda Parte (Manila: La Imprenta de la Compania de Jesus, 1749), Lib. III, Cap. 15, p. 278.

It is safer to conclude that the people described here were the inland or mountain people of Mindoro. These were thus the same people that the Jesuits began to evangelize.

The Jesuits' efforts at converting the Mangyans were not without results for Colin records that a few years after they took spiritual charge of the island, "some 600 of the tribe...received Baptism."[12] Such conversions took place around the area of present-day Naujan where the first Jesuit residence was located.

Though the initial number of tribal members converted to the Faith is quite impressive, the Catholic mission among the Mangyans progressed rather slowly. For one thing, the mission was racked by keen rivalry between the seculars and the Jesuits. Zealous and unflagging in their religious labor, the Jesuits in a short period of time outshone the seculars' work in Mindoro. Consequently, the seculars turned against their former agreement with the Jesuits. Contesting the Jesuits' presence in the Mindoro mission, the seculars sought the law and as a result, Mindoro was returned to the latter group. However, the seculars appeared to be more interested in preserving their territorial hold than in the religious evangelization of the Mangyans. In the words of Domingo Navarrete, the seculars considered the island as "the things that they own, and not the things that are Jesus Christ's." This highly materialistic view of an otherwise religious venture inevitably led to the stagnation of the work. For 15 years there was a lull in religious activity in Mindoro, broken only by a revival of missionary activity in 1665. Significantly, the ones who led the revival campaigns were the Jesuits.

Velarde records that in October of the year 1665, which also saw a violent earthquake hit Manila, Fray Diego Luis de San Vitores and some companions undertook a missionary trip to Mindoro.[13] He notes down the difficulty of their travels but observes that the "time and strength were well spent for not only the old Christians (lowlanders) were revived in their faith but... the infidel Mangyans, many of whom were converted to (our) religion."[14]

---

[12] From the translation of sections of Colin's work, *op. cit.*, Lib. I, Cap. 16, p. 64.

[13] Velarde, *op. cit.*, in B & R, Vol. 44, p. 103.

[14] *Ibid.* Another report of the same mission cites that the fathers were able to instruct and baptize about 500 Mangyans whom they reduced to settlements near the existing Tagalog and Visayan villages. Altogether, the mission resulted in the establishment of three new Mangyan villages. Cf. "Missiones del Colegio de la Compañia de Jesus de Manila desde Julio de 1665 hasta la quaresma de

Domingo Navarrete, apparently a member of the team, records a very fruitful campaign though it lasted only for the dry season. Apart from its importance as a document of the Church's growth in Mindoro, Navarrete's account presents very enlightening facts about the ethnology of the coastal and interior peoples of this period. The perceptive friar explicitly differentiates between the "negrillos" of the mountain and the indios of the coasts.

An interesting feature of Navarrete's account is the already-existing consciousness of class differences between the lowland indios and the Mangyans. To the Tagalog coastal dwellers, the Mangyans were wild people thriving on scavenging for food. Navarrete gives us this impression in what follows:

> ...the Indians, having finished with the carabao, left these (Negrillos) there with the intestines, stomach and bones. The Indians told me that, after our party would leave the place, all these wild people would gather here, and would not go away until they had gnawed the bones, and would even eat the stomach with its contents.[15]

Another equally significant fact that Navarrete refers to in his work is the growing menace of the *Camucones* in Mindoro. On his second mission to Mindoro, the warm-hearted Jesuit noted the disconsolate state of the people of Naujan whose chief was captured by the piratical group from south of the Philippines. Noted for its prosperity, the town of Naujan became a favorite prey of the pirates from Borneo.

The missionary activities of the priests, who rekindled the Catholic faith in the island, included instruction, preaching, hearing confessions and settling their affairs. Many conversions and revivals of special interest were made among the Christian lowlanders and Mangyans. Velarde in particular cites the conversion of a Mangyan woman,

> ...a heathen, married to a Christian man. She was baptized, and named Maria; and afterward they called her "the Samaritana," on account of the many persons whom she brought to the knowledge of Christ, the ministers availing themselves of her aid for the conversions of many persons, not only heathens but Christians, with most happy results.[16]

Velarde's account brings out several matters of great import. For one thing, it tells of intermarriage between a Mangyan and a "Chris-

---

1666," *ibid.*, 12, as cited in H. de la Costa, *The Jesuits in the Philippines, 1581–1768*. (Cambridge, Mass.: Harvard University Press, 1961), p. 473-74.

[15] Domingo Navarrete, O.P.: 1676. "Manila and the Philippines about 1650" (concluded). B & R, Vol. 38, 1674-1683, p. 28.

[16] Velarde, *op. cit.*, p. 104.

tian man," undoubtedly indicating a close lowland-Mangyan interaction, which is also reflected in the acceptance of the woman as a witness of the Faith. The fact that the priests used her not only to facilitate conversion of the Mangyans but also of lowlanders would mean her acceptance into lowland culture. The distinction made between "Mangyan" and "Christian man" should however be underlined, as this possibly reflects the growing differentiation between a developing lowland "Christian culture" and the traditional highland culture. This may further be inferred from the account that follows:

> In order to convert these heathens, a beginning was made by the reformation and instruction of the Christians (i.e., lowlanders); and by frequent preaching they gradually established the usage of confession with some frequency, and many received the Eucharist—a matter in which there was more difficulty then than now. Many came down from the mountains, and brought their children to be instructed; various persons were baptized, and even some, who, although they had the name of Christians, had never received the rite of baptism. After the fathers preached to the Christians regarding honesty in their confessions, the result was quickly seen in many general confessions, which were made with such eagerness that the crowds resorting to the church lasted more than two months.[17]

The religious revival that the Jesuits started in the island was quite evidently extensive. The adoption of Christian names, the willingness to be baptized and to have the children taught by the friars show the extent of the compelling influence or religious pressure exerted by the Spanish priests on the Mangyans with whom they came in contact.

As a further consequence of the religious revival, three churches were erected for the converted Mangyans: one in Bongabon, another in Pola, and still another in San Javier on the coast of Naujan.[18] Velarde adds that a church was also built for the holy Christ of

---

[17] *Ibid.* The chief obstacle to the conversion of the Mangyans as the friars themselves found out was that the lowland Christians did not particularly want them to settle down, as they were much more of use to them as ignorant "tribesmen" whom they could send into the forest for wild bees wax or employ as "slaves" in their farms. Apparently, the missionaries' exhortations were so effective that the Christians themselves went to the hills, sought out their Mangyan "serfs," brought them down to be instructed by the fathers, fed and housed them while they were being prepared for baptism. Cf. "Annual Letter of the Jesuit Philippine Province for 1622," and Missiones de la Compania de Jesus cited in de la Costa, *Ibid.*, p. 375-76, 473-74.

[18] M. Velarde, *op. cit.*, p. 104.

Burgos, for those old Christians "who were roaming about through the mountains."[19] Whether this refers to old Christian Mangyans or to lowlanders who had gone nomadic is not clear from Velarde's account.

To sum up, compelling religious influence exerted by the pioneer Spanish missionaries in Mindoro forms one of the earliest pressures on Mangyan life. However, this should not be set apart from the equally compelling force provided by the Spanish colonial government which came simultaneously with the Cross.

EFFECTS OF SPANISH COLONIAL RULE IN MINDORO

Before the institution of Spanish rule throughout the Philippine Islands, a convenient means through which the Spaniards brought their sovereignty directly to the villages was through intermittent *entradas*—procurement raids some of which were also exploratory or punitive in character. In Mindoro, Ilin and Lubang, Salcedo's punitive expeditions netted the Spaniards many spoils of war. Likewise, in the Bicol Region, Captain Enriquez de Guzman's pacification not only allowed his friar companion, Alonzo Jimenez, to evangelize and maintain Spanish sovereignty in Masbate (with a garrison of only six soldados) but also helped sustain the entire Spanish expedition. These entradas seem to have been a normal fare for the military community seeking survival in a hostile area. This was resorted to before the pacified lands were divided into encomiendas.

The encomienda system was a device to collect tributes from the indigenes, and was in effect an attempt on the part of the Spanish colonizers to reach the native base.[20] Through encomiendas, the slowly arising colonial state tried to introduce effective control over the newly-acquired territories and to systematically extract sustenance from the countryside. This system so conceived could be royal or private. In this light, it was the private encomienda which readily became a source of tension in the evolving colonial state.

---

[19] *Ibid.* Fr. de la Costa identifies these as the *cimarrons*, "that is, Christians who for various reasons had fled to the hills and were now persuaded to return to civilization." *Ibid.*, p. 473.

[20] For a more thorough study of this set-up, consult A. M. Avellana, "The Encomienda System in the Philippines," M.A. thesis (M.L.Q.U., 1953); J. C. Foster, "The Encomienda System in the Philippines, 1571-1597," M.A. thesis (Loyola University, 1956); and Helen Tubangui, "The Encomienda as a Social and Economic Institution in the Philippines," M.A. thesis (Ateneo, 1956).

In theory, the encomienda was a triangular system of relations among the King, the encomendero and the natives, with the royal right to collect tribute from the natives delegated to the encomendero who, in return, was to render military service to the crown, make his wards accept Spanish sovereignty, defend their lives and properties, and provide them with a minimum of religious instruction. There was, however, a fourth party to the supposed agreement—the friar missionary. The friar also had a stake in the tribute, for it was from the encomendero's collection that the mission was to be subsidized. Thus, some concerned friars, like Fray Martin de Rada, condemned the method of collection and consequent selfish use of tribute, but nevertheless favored its continuance since they were also dependent on it for support. As such, the Filipinos not only lost their freedom but were also made to finance their own political subjugation and their own Christianization. In truth, the Spaniards lived on the sweat and blood of their encomienda wards.

The abuses of the tribute and the slavery attendant to the *encomiendas de particulares,* which the ambivalent friars denounced, eventually led to some changes that called for the extension of the system of *alcaldes mayores* over the encomiendas. In this innovation, the *alcalde mayor* was meant to be in an official place directly above the encomenderos in a supervisory capacity. Thus, within this setup, the encomienda in Mindoro, as described by Retana, was not only under religious administration but also under the "chief magistrate" residing in Balayan. Retana's *relacion* cites that the encomienda in "Vaco, Mindoro" belonging to Philippe de Saucedo consisted of 700 tributaries with about 2,800 persons.

In 1591, Mindoro was separated from the province of Batangas and was organized into a *corregimiento* with Puerto Galera as the capital. Under this system, the island was placed under a military officer called the *corregidor,* but as Teodoro Agoncillo points out, conditions of peace and order were less stable under such order.[21] In 1663, a change took place in the form of administration in the island. The corregidor was replaced by the alcalde-mayor or provincial governor and the capital was moved to Baco. Colin records that in the year:

---

[21] Teodoro A. Agoncillo and Oscar M. Alfonso, *History of the Filipino People,* (Quezon City: Malaya Books, 1967), p. 86.

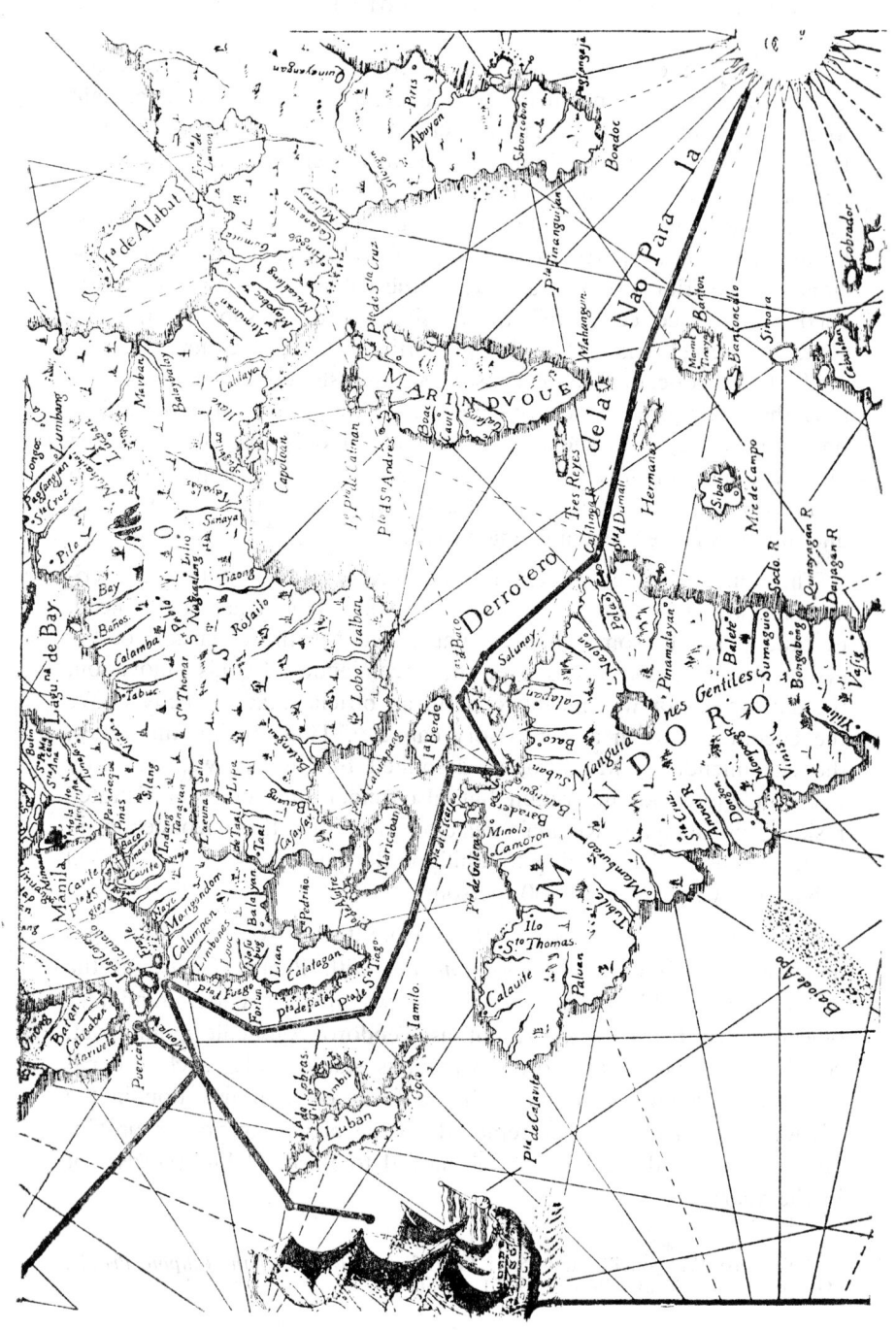

Mindoro as charted in Fr. Pedro M. Velarde's map (1743)

> La cabecera de la Isla, y jurisdicion en que reside el Alcalde mayor, es Baco, pueblo de saludables aguas, porllevar los montes, en que nace surio, la sarsaparilla: bien, que no tan fina como de la Castilla.[22]

Under the new system, the alcalde mayor or provincial governor was the chief political, judicial, financial and military official.[23] This concentration of power in the hands of the same official inevitably led to abuse of power. Thus until the reform decrees of 1844 and 1886 introduced some changes, there were four principal sources of abuses by the alcalde-mayor: the exercise of judicial powers, the collection of tributes, the privilege to engage in commerce, and the lending of money. Agoncillo points out further that

> At the same time that he was the highest executive official in the province, the alcalde-mayor was also the highest judicial official and performed the functions of a judge of first instance. The anomalous nature of this arrangement derives from the fact that some of those who became alcaldes-mayores were formerly hair-dressers, lackeys, sailors, or deserters, with no background in the law. One who was himself ignorant about the law performed the duty of interpreting the law... As the only judge in the province, the alcalde-mayor was in the enviable position of making the decision himself.[24]

The abuses perpetrated by the alcaldes-mayores reached a point where the Spanish military and naval officers themselves had to take action to stop them from making business out of official functions:

> ... Se quitó a los alcalde mayores toda attribucios en materia de corso, para evitar el abuso de que utilizasen en provecho propio'y en sus negocios commerciales de los buques del Estado, y es mando' reparar todos los fuertes de los Visayas, Mindoro, Tayabas y Zamboanga.[25]

Despite the establishment of such an oppressive system, the isle of Mindoro remained a flourishing port for some time. Antonio de Morga, a noted and well-respected historian of the 17th century, includes it in his list "of the more extensive, and the principal and best known islands in the country." [26]

He gives a concise description of Mindoro, and points out that it has many settlements of natives similar to those found in other is-

---

[22] Colin, *op. cit.*, p. 27.
[23] Agoncillo and Alfonso, *op. cit.*, p. 86.
[24] *Ibid.*
[25] D. Jose Montero y Vidal, *Historia de la Pirateria Malayo-Mohametana en Mindanao Jolo y Borneo*, Tomo I (Madrid: Imprenta y Fundecion de Manuel Tellos, 1888), p. 350.
[26] Antonio de Morga, *Sucesos de las Islas Filipinas* trans. by Encarnacion Alzona and annotated by Jose Rizal (Manila: Jose Rizal Centennial Commission, 1962), p. 267.

lands. These people, according to him, "settle on the side where it bounds with the province of Balayan (Batangas) and Calilaya." Apart from these, Morga identifies a principal settlement in the island which has a port called the *Varadero* or shipyard for large vessels, aside from other places of anchorage and sand-bars for smaller vessels. He also records many other settlements of natives all along the coast of the island, all of which localities, according to him, abounded in rice and food supplies.[27]

THE MUSLIM "PIRATICAL" MOVES IN MINDORO

The relative prosperity of the coastal towns of Mindoro met a serious setback with the rise of Muslim "piracy" in the 17th century. While Professor Majul asserts that not all "Moro" attacks at that time were purely piratical, he acknowledges the existence of Muslim marauders carrying out "their private enterprises."[28] It is primarily these "private piratical groups" that were instrumental in bringing about the deterioration of the coastal towns of Mindoro. Barely a century after the onset of piratical attacks on Mindoro, the island was greatly depopulated and was reduced to a malaria-infested region, devastated and stripped of all its former prosperity.

From several Spanish accounts, it is possible to infer many sidelights of the actions of the pirates in Mindoro. Montero y Vidal's *Historia de Pirateria,* Vicente Barrantes' *Guerras Piraticas de Filipinas* and a number of other Spanish writings become highly relevant on this count. In recent times, Prof. Majul's *Muslims in the Philippines* provides new perspectives on these long-drawn conflicts between the "Moros" and Spaniards.

Yet, regardless of Majul's redefinition of the Moro wars and the effort to re-interpret three centuries of Muslim attacks on various Spanish-held territories at that time, the fact remains that such struggles constituted at one point a tremendous pressure on the lives of the inhabitants of those places. Taken as captives and sold as slaves, at times killed mercilessly, the natives were innocent "pawns" caught in the conflict between the Spaniards and the Muslims. In the final analysis, the natives of the islands and not the Spaniards were the ones who truly bore the brunt of Muslim assaults.

[27] *Op. cit.*
[28] Majul, *op. cit.,* p. 108.

The first recorded Muslim attack of Mindoro took place in 1602 when a Maguindanao fleet led by Datu Buisan attacked the island and some coastal towns of Luzon, as part of a larger Islamic offensive against the Spanish presence in the country. According to the existing accounts, the Muslims scourged the coastal town of Mindoro and a few settlements in Luzon and netted about 700 captives including clergymen.[29] Majority of the captives were of course natives who later on were turned into slaves or exchanged for goods. According to Majul, captives were taken to weaken inhabitants of "Spanish-held territories fighting the Muslims, to provide income to the raiders (as the practice was to exact huge ransoms from Spanish officials, native chieftains or men of importance), and to strengthen the war machine of the Muslims, as well as to increase their agricultural production," the captives being kept not only as household retainers but also as farm or agricultural workers to enable the Muslims and the other so-called freemen to dedicate themselves to the profession of fighting.[30] Fray Martinez de Zuñiga further records that while the captives had not yet reached the homes of the Moros, they suffered great hardships. According to him, the Christian captives

>...are placed in wooden stocks, at times with both feet and hands inserted, and safely tied so that they could not escape. When the business of the sales and barter of captives are over, they enjoy greater freedom and are often ordered to serve in their master's house and to get water, to catch fish, and other chores...[31]

Another recorded Muslim attack on Mindoro took place in April 1636, when Tagal, the kapitan-laut of Sultan Qudarat set forth to spend a season of plundering in Mindoro and Calamianes. On this expedition, the Spanish captain Juan Lopez writes that Tagal

>...went to Mindoro, and everywhere he pillaged a great quantity of goods, and took a number of captives. He left Don Diego Alabes in Mindoro (he was assigned as corregidor in Cuyo and Palawan) so that he might come (here) to get ransom and that of the three Recollect fathers. They demanded two thousand pesos and thirty taels of gold—the latter amounting to more than 300 pesos in addition for each person.[32]

---
[29] *Ibid.*, p. 117.
[30] *Ibid.*, p. 122.
[31] Fr. Joaquin Martinez de Zuñiga, *Estadismo de las Islas Filipinas o Mis Viajes por Esta Pais*. Tomo Primero (Madrid: Dec. 1893), p. 110.
[32] Juan Lopez, "Events in the Philippines," in B & R, Vol. 27, pp. 136-37; 316.

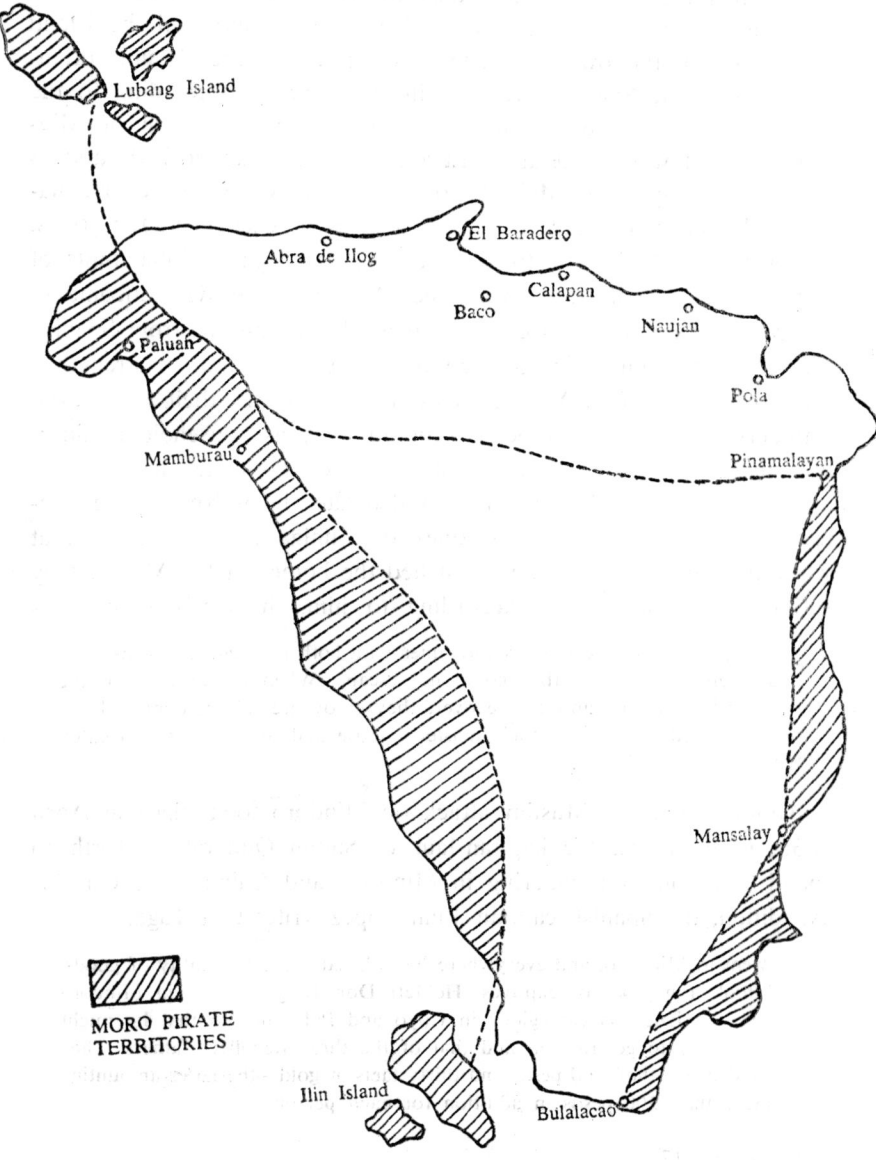

"Moro Pirate" territories in Mindoro during the 18th and early 19th centuries.

According to another account which Blair and Robertson assume to be that of Pedro Gutierrez, S.J. in 1637, Tagal remained almost eight months in the coast of Mindoro, "robbing and inflicting enormous damage." [33] In 1657 the Moro chief, Balatamay, was reported to have committed the most terrible atrocities in the islands of Marinduque and Mindoro, returning to Mindanao with much booty and a multitude of captives. Montero y Vidal's account provides a more graphic account of Balatamay's incursions in Luzon. According to this historian, Balatamay's

> ... boldness brought them as far as the coast of Mariveles, near Manila in whose waters he seized two Chinese vessels filled with goods. Upon their return they stayed in Mamburao, an island of Mindoro, where they built a hidden factory, where some traders went to make business and from whence they (the Moros) sold their native captives.[34]

Though the Spaniards undertook several expeditions against the Muslims, the latter were able to hold on to their fortified strongholds for centuries, and to carry on their "pillaging business" in the Christian areas. Towards this end, Mindoro served as a convenient base and stop-over for the Muslim pirates. Further accounts of Muslim action in Mindoro report that in 1753 and 1754 Calapan, the capital of Mindoro, was sacked and burned to the ground. In the first raid, 409 prisoners were taken and an unknown number in the second. At an earlier date, in 1726, Manaol, near Mansalay, was destroyed. In 1754 they took 150 prisoners between Bongabong and Bulalacao areas which until recently were recorded as Hanunoo settlements.

In 1762, a Spanish expedition of 1,250 men was sent from Manila against the Muslims, who had fortified themselves on a peninsula between the rivers Maasin and Mamburao. It momentarily checked Muslim activity in the region. An apparent recurrence of piratical incursions in the years that followed led to the sending of an even larger force in 1778. This expedition, led by a certain Don Jose Gomez, went to relieve Mamburao which had been reoccupied by the pirates after they had burned the town as well as boats and crops. In this, Gomez was ironically duplicating the exploit of Juan de Salcedo who did exactly the same thing in 1570. The expedition was

---
[33] *Ibid.*, p. 215.
[34] Montero y Vidal, *op. cit.*, p. 333.

apparently successful for, as Montero y Vidal writes, "commerce started to progress (i.e., for the Spaniards), except in Samar whose trade relations with Manila were paralyzed for more than ten years."[35] Subsequently, the Spaniards successively made more assaults in other places, particularly in Balete which the Muslims frequented, but, because they always had easy access to the mountains, the Spanish expeditions did not produce the desired effect.

The successive Muslim raids and Spanish counter-attacks staged in Mindoro inevitably led to the destruction of formerly flourishing coastal towns and the depopulation of such places, for numerous inhabitants were taken as captives, or were forced to flee inland to relative safety. In 1800, Fray Joaquin de Zuñiga, who traveled through Mindoro, recounted that the coves of Pinamalayan and other places in Mindoro which used to be populated had become entirely deserted and had been transformed into hiding places of pirates. Of Ilin, a former Spanish gold dust claim, Zuñiga wrote that neither houses nor people could be seen "because the Moros have wrought havoc on the region and have settled down there."[36] The noted Spanish writer likewise avers that in his time the pirates could no longer undertake the "piratical expeditions of yesteryears, nor could they rob anymore to their hearts' content."[37]

An anonymous writer, whose local knowledge must have been great, states that previous to the devastating piratical assaults, the island was well-peopled and cultivated. In fact, he notes that the vestiges of their former prosperity were still to be met in his time (i.e., circa 1848). Among the significant facts he mentions were the abundance of rice production and the existence of a wide variety of rice species. These references prove that Mindoro was indeed "the granary of the Islands" before the piratical incursions.

The unknown writer further observes that the presence of many ruins of formerly magnificent church structures in extraordinary places such as the one found on a narrow plain called "Punta de Sto. Tomas" on the north coast between Abra de Ilog and Calavite Point proves how rich and populous the island of Mindoro must have been in former times. In the words of the writer, "their roads of communication

---

[35] *Ibid.*, p. 360.
[36] *Ibid.*, p. 110.
[37] *Ibid.*

with other inhabited places must have employed great intelligence and immense labor." However, all these seem to have been "labour lost," considering the bloody and destructive invasion of the pirates.

Greatly perturbed about the desolate state of Mindoro in his time, our anonymous writer notes:

> How is it that a country so extensive, so rich in natural productions, and so near Manila and to the populous and industrious island of Panay, can thus be deserted? It can be owing to the frequent incursions of the pirate Moors, to the insalubrity of many of the districts from their uncultivated state, but most of all to the excess of territory in proportion to the population which exists throughout this Archipelago.[38]

While a decline in piratical incursions was noted in this period, existing accounts also cite sporadic "Moro attacks" even towards the end of the 19th century. Jordana, for instance, records raids made as late as 1870 and 1874 in places listed as Bulalacao (which Gardner at the start of the 20th century identified as a Hanunoo region), Tulin and Socol.[39] Including these last raids, Muslim "piratical" activities in Mindoro cover almost three centuries of known suffering and pain.

It is evident from the foregoing accounts that the population of Mindoro went through tremendous strain for centuries. Without doubt, the consistent burning of towns either by the "Moro pirates" or the rampaging Spaniards, the ransacking of homes and capture of natives for the slave market could very well have brought Mindoro to its end as a port of major importance. A further effect must have been to drive the population either into exile in safer places or to send them inland to comparative safety. Joseph Montano, a Frenchman who traveled through the Philippines during this period, brings out this point vividly in his account:

> ... As for the big island of Mindoro, situated more towards the southwest, it was in olden days the granary of the Philippines. Mindoro was colonized by the Fathers of the Company of Jesus; in the preceding century, the suppression of the Company gave a fatal blow to its prosperity; *the raids of the Moros finalized its ruin* (italics mine, V.B.L). Today, the Tagalog population, very small, is more or less concentrated on the shores. Some

---

[38] The Spanish original of this translation was probably written August-September 1848 or even earlier. The translation appears in the *Journal of the Indian Archipelago and Eastern Asia* (Singapore), Series I, Vol. 3 (1849), pp. 765-66.

[39] Ramon Morera Jordana *Bosquejo Geografico e Historico Natural del Archipelago Filipino* (Madrid Impr. de Moreno y Reyes, 1885), p. 52.

half-savage Manguianes who some say are of the same race as the Tagalogs, roam in the thick forest which covers the ruins of formerly flourishing towns.[40]

It is interesting to note that while the Spanish accounts strongly attribute the destruction of Mindoro to Muslim attacks, Montano places the blame largely on the Spaniards' mismanagement of the affairs of the island. Rizal himself assumed this view and in his annotation of Morga's work writes with sarcasm,

> Mindoro is so depopulated that the Minister of Overseas Colonies, in order to remedy this effect of the Spanish colonization, wants to send to that island the most dissolute from Spain to see if great beasts can be made into good settlers and farmers. Anyway, considering the condition of the people who are going there, undoubtedly the following generation will know how to defend themselves and live so that the island will not be depopulated again.[41]

Thus, along with the disastrous effect of Muslim piracy, the Spanish exaction of heavy tributes among the inhabitants, the imposition of burdensome monopolies, and the unreasonable requirement of forced services in the forts contributed equally to the deterioration of Mindoro. Fray de Zuñiga himself recognized such abuses and strongly advised that the Spaniards would have no hope of seeing the island populated again and prospering, unless

> ... the people be exempted from paying the required tribute for several years until such a time when some regular towns could have been established, that they would not abandon their houses, that no monopolies be imposed on them nor burden them with the forced services in the forts—unless so needed for their own security. If to these measures of gentleness and indifference to profit are substituted severity and covetousness, no progress shall be expected... If the magistrate starts to collect tribute with harshness, if they ask that they be paid in kind—made burdensome with the imposition of value exceeding one-half of the regular peso—if the guards commit their usual wanton tricks with the pretext of listing down the smuggled goods, if the magistrates would once again bother the native merchants by extorting from them the little profit they make, they will easily go to places where they will be treated with consideration and respect.[42]

Mass immigration to nearby provinces like Batangas served, at one point, as a handy means of escape from the rampaging Muslims and

---

[40] Joseph Montano, *Voyage Aux Philippines Et. En, Malaisie* (Paris: Hachett, 1886), p. 78. Translation by Dr. Zeus A. Salazar.
[41] Jose Rizal's annotation to Morga's *Sucesos de las Islas Filipinas, op. cit.*
[42] de Zuñiga, *op. cit.*, p. 112.

the tyrannical Spanish magistrates. Zuñiga records that about 1,165 families migrated to Batangas in 1735 to evade such menaces.

THE MANGYANS IN THE 19TH CENTURY

Despite their relative isolation, the Mangyans were not fully free from the "Moro" piratical incursions. As a matter of fact, the Muslim pirates found safe refuge in the interior when faced with overwhelming Spanish forces. Zuñiga writes that such easy access to the mountains made it impossible for the Spanish soldiers "to hunt them like wolves and deer." On such occasions when pirates freely roamed in the interior, Mangyan villages were raided and consequently destroyed. This apparently conditioned the Mangyans to flee at the slightest awareness of the presence of strangers, fearing they were pirates. In the mountains, according to Zuñiga, the fleeing native captives "usually come in contact with heathen natives who reside there and *who usually flee upon seeing them, thinking that they might be "Moros" who did plenty of harm many times before*" (italics mine— V.B.L.).

Apart from the pirates, the Christian captives who managed to escape from them also fled to the interior of Mindoro and came in close contact with the Mangyans.

> In order to persuade these pagans that they are peaceful men who need their help, continues Zuñiga, "these Christian escapees kneel down before the mountaineers and arrange their arms in the form of a cross," which, recognized as a signal, becomes the occasion for the *infieles* to "take them to their home and entertain them."[43]

It is possible that such captives taken from different parts of Luzon intermarried with the Mangyans and maintained residence among them—possibly contributing to the growing diversification of the inland culture.

In truth, the anonymous writer of 1848 records that those few individuals who escaped from the Moros congregated in the neighborhood of the savage tribe that was known to have inhabited the central mountains from time immemorial and whose district, lying in the northern part of Mindoro, was designated by the indios as "Banguu."[44] The writer presents an interesting theory which sup-

---

[43] *Ibid.*

[44] This term may be the derivative of "Bangon" used even to this day to refer to the least exposed Mangyan group occupying the same area cited by the anonymous writer.

poses that the descendants of these fugitives were "the people who now constitute the interior population of Mindoro, independent of the Spanish authority and who are distinguished by the generic name 'Manguianes.'" Significantly, the well-informed writer differentiates between the "Manguianes" and the "primitive tribe Banguu" who spoke a different idiom. He adds that after the first moments of panic were over, the "Manguianes" separated from the Banguu, relating "a thousand fantastic tales about the customs of this mountain tribe, and have left them alone and isolated in their lurking places."

These "Manguianes" may well be the ancestors of the Buhids and Hanunoos today. In a study made by this writer of some of the Buhid oral literature, faint references to the "Moros" in their *urukay* were discovered. The urukay is a rhythmic poetic expression which the Buhids distinguish from the *ambahan*. The "Moro" strains in the urukay may be gleaned from what follows:

> May naglutaw sakayan
> Atibay kantam sugdaan
> Bukot bata kamurusan
> Batang kabundukan.
>
> (There appeared a vessel
> There in our travel path
> But fear need not stalk your heart,
> For they are not real 'Moros'
> but only mountain folks.)

Somehow, through the long years of the bloody and destructive piratical assaults, the ancient Mangyans may have transmitted to their descendants the panicky terror which the "Moros" excited in them—the convenient vehicle being the urukay, rhythmic recitations meant to teach and entertain the Buhids of today.

Apart from the difference in religion, no significant distinctions between lowlanders and Mangyans are set forth early in the 19th century. In 1800, Fray de Zuñiga described them simply as the "non-Christians of Mindoro" who "are natives like the others, but... (being) less exposed to civilizing influences... like a more miserable life."

The miseries of the Mangyans came in the form of lowland exploitation. As the well-respected Spanish historian perceived it,

> The Christians give them a bolo and rice to plant. What they do is to burn a piece of barren land (possibly a kaingin—V.B.L.) and with the bolo they plant the rice; when reaping time comes he gives back

one-half of his harvest in return for the bolo and the seeds. He might have to give up the whole harvest if he had back dues. The more fortunate people of Mindanao (*sic*) take too much advantage of their non-Christian fellows. They buy the honey and wax gathered by the Mangyans in the forest at a low price and sell or barter them with goods from Manila priced exorbitantly, which yield them much profit. This is one of the reasons why these gentiles do not desire to be baptized or to embrace the Catholic faith even if the priest instruct them in Christianity and even if they often visit the Christian towns.[45]

Setting aside his bias, Zuñiga's observation presents a keen view of lowland-Mangyan interaction at the start of the 19th century. As will be shown later on, almost the same form of exploitation of the Mangyans exists to this day, thus proving the long history of lowland abuse of the Mangyan people. It is ironic but true to this day that the nominally Christian lowlanders are themselves the deterrents to the total conversion of these "tribal" peoples to the Christian faith. The Spanish ecclesiastical policy to remedy such a situation is summed up in Zuñiga's pronouncement that all these difficulties "will be remedied if evangelical ministers are placed in the hinterland, independent of other towns, and if new towns are organized for those who are newly converted."[46]

The policy of setting up new towns for "converted pagans" was a widespread Spanish practice in dealing with the "heathen" people of the country. Such a practice was considered by Felix Keesing as a major key to the cultural differentiation which developed between "Christian lowland" Filipino and the mountain people. The noted anthropologist believed that

With pacification and Hispanization of the lowland groups, and resistance by the mountain groups, the lines were drawn between Christian and non-Christian, which were to last up to modern times. At most, mission workers were able to whittle away at the edge of the mountain populations, transferring them down to the lowland communities.[47]

If one is to accept Keesing's thesis and there is a strong ground for it, it would appear that the northern lowland and highland peoples are basically of the same racial stock. Inferring from the existing Spanish accounts, the same thing could be said of the indigenes of Mindoro. Language-wise, several Spanish accounts remark that the inhabitants

---

[45] *Ibid.*, p. 120.
[46] *Ibid.*
[47] Felix M. Keesing, *The Ethnohistory of Northern Luzon* (Stanford, California: Stanford University Press, 1962), p. 27.

Distribution of the Mangyan tribes in Mindoro in the 19th century.

of Mindoro, Marinduque and Lubang "speak Tagalog which is the official language of the whole archbishopric of Manila which has jurisdiction over these islands."[48] He adds that in the way they build their houses and furniture, in their method of dressing, in the appearance of their boats, and in their habits and customs, they were similar to their Tagalog brothers. In what appears to be a pioneer ethnological account of the Mangyans in relation to their lowland brothers, Zuñiga wrote that:

> The Christians of the three islands believe in the same superstitions of the Tagalogs and the infidels believe in the same religion of the Tagalogs before their conversion to Catholicism.
> All of them adore an invisible entity called anito whose name is likewise given to the thing sacrificed to him.
> All of them adore the Nono or spirit of his ancestors, whom they respect and revere in the form of an alligator, big trees, stones, and the end of all rivers and seas.
> All of them have priestesses who offer the sacrifices for (sic) them, this sacrifice may be a whole pig which is divided reserving the better portion to the priestess or babaylan. They even revere some birds, believe in the immortality of the soul, and at the same time believe all the superstitions of the ancient gentiles of these islands...[49]

Until late in the 19th century, the Mangyans were known as a homogeneous people. One of the first men to contest such a view is Ramon Morera Jordana, a Spanish historian and naturalist who came out with a detailed study of the Mangyans in 1885. Among other things, Jordana notes how the Mangyans set themselves apart from the Buquiles, a half-breed tribe belonging to the Negrito race and who inhabited the area near Baco and Subaan. The Mangyans themselves were classified by Jordana into three ethnic groupings:

(1) those who occupy the Occidental coast of the Island, occupying the mountains in Palauan to Irurun. They are fair complexioned and of intelligent physiognomy (intelligent-looking), have thick brown hair and beard, robust and graceful, and peaceful.
(2) those who inhabit the territories between Abra de Ilog and Pinamalayan are tan in complexion, with wavy hair (lit. flacid), prominent cheekbones, flat forehead, somewhat long-nosed (?) and dull-looking.
(3) those who inhabit that part of Pinamalayan until the South look as if they are of Chinese blood, not only because of their oblique

---
[48] de Zuñiga, op. cit., p. 121
[49] Ibid., p. 122.

eyes, flat nose, prominent cheekbones, flat forehead and olive skin, but also of their custom of having a long braid in the upper part of their head with the rest of their hair if not shaved, cut short. This tribe who are quite hard-working, judging by the products that they bring to the Christian towns, are undoubtedly less poor than the two other breeds.[50]

The third group, based on its habitat and other ethnological data given by Jordana, is the Hanunoo tribe of today.

Further, Jordana points out that the names with which the given ethnic types distinguish themselves are rather vague:

> Between Socol and Bulalacao, the name Manguianes is used for the pagans who live in the shore of the rivers. Those who stay in the lowlands are called Buquil and Beribi, to those who are found sheltered in the peak of the mountains. In Pinamalayan, they call the inhabitants of the same localities given above as Bangot, Buquit, Tadianan and Durugman or Buctulan respectively. In Naujan, they substitute the last name for Tiron (those who live in the mountain peaks) and from this part until Abra de Ilog, they use only the generic name of Manguian. Lastly in Mangarin, they call Lactan those who stay in the lowlands, Buquil, those who dwell in the river shores, Manguian those who reside in the mountain slopes and Barangan (possibly the Batangans or Tawbuids today) those who inhabit the peaks of the mountain ranges.[51]

It is evident from Jordana's work that he understood "Manguian" as a collective term encompassing several ethnic groups of very different origins. Blumentritt, the time-honored Austrian scholar who translated and annotated Jordana's work in German, affirms that the latter's description of the *Buquiles* "reveals without doubt that the group is the result of a cross between the latter (i.e., the "negrito race") and the indios, that is to say natives of Malay origin."[52] Blumentritt further believes that the term Buquil may mean "mountain," as, for instance, in the root word of the ethnic name of *Bukidnon*. As for the name Tiron cited above, it may refer, according to him, to the remnants of pirates who came from the island of Tawi-Tawi, as well as from the area of Tiron (Tedun, Tidon) in the island

[50] *Ibid.*
[51] *Ibid.*, p. 54.
[52] From Ferdinand Blumentritt, "Die Manguianen del Insel Mindoro (Philippinen)," *Globus*, Vol. 50 (4886), footnote 3, p. 216. Translation by Dr. Zeus A. Salazar. Blumentritt's article is an annotated translation of R. Jordana Y. Morera's previously mentioned account of the Mangyans.

of Borneo.[53] Indeed, such differences in ethnic origins may well be attributed to the varying groups of people who migrated to Mindoro at different periods of its history. The Buquiles may well be the descendants of those lowlanders already mentioned who escaped from the Moro pirates, found safety and refuge among the interior Negrito inhabitants, and intermarried with them.

Due to the diverse ethnic groupings of the Mangyans, ethnographers of the period were indecisive about classifying them as "a people." As Ferdinand Blumentritt writes, the Mangyans of his time

> ... are in fact a very little known people. If in point of fact they constitute a people, for it is assumed that the name Mangyan which means as much as "forest men" (people) is a general name for all pagans, excepting those with full negrito blood, who live in the interior of that big island.[54]

While they were generally considered by Spanish and other European writers as "half-savages" with a very low level of culture, the Mangyans were nonetheless shown to be in possession of a script of their own. This fact surprised some European scholars like Blumentritt himself who, commenting on Dr. Adolf Bernhard Meyer and Dr. A. Schadenberg's work,[55] wrote:

> From the materials given ... we can only see that the Mangyans are on a very low level of culture and civilization. One was therefore very little prepared to discover a script in such a people.[56]

Though the existence of the Mangyan script was known to some Spanish and even Filipino writers like Pedro A. Paterno, the extent of their writings on the subject was very minimal. Paterno, who came up with a few lines about it in his book *Los Aetas,* was in the words of Meyer as cited by Blumentritt, "even unaware of the importance

---

[53] During the first half of the 17th century, the so-called *Camucones* from Borneo generally made "follow-up" raids in the manner of vultures after the Sulus had committed their depredations. Even after north Borneo was ceded to the Sulus around the 1680s, it took them still at least a century of intermittent expeditions to subdue the *Camucones* (cf. Majul, *op. cit.,* pp. 123, 125, 127, *passim* and Velarde, *op. cit.,* pp. 43-44, *passim*). Thus, Borneo (or a part of this big island) may have indeed been involved in the ethnic history of Mindoro—at any rate, in relation to the so-called "Moro Wars."

[54] Ferdinand Blumentritt, "Die Mangianenschrift von Mindoro," *Globus,* Vol. 69, 1896, p. 21, translated by Dr. Zeus A. Salazar.

[55] See A. B. Meyer, A. Schadenberg, "Die Mangianenschrift von Mindoro," Berlin, R. Friedlander, 1895.

[56] Ferdinand Blumentritt, *op. cit.,* "Die Mangianenschrift von Mindoro."

of his discovery."⁵⁷ To Blumentritt, in fact, Paterno's reference to the Mangyan script "is almost without value since it shows simply that the Mangyans have a script of their own." ⁵⁸ On the other hand, Blumentritt further opined, the Spanish friars "to whom we owe so many grammars and vocabularies of Philippine idioms have not unfortunately given any attention to the Mangyans."⁵⁹

The first scholar who came up with really substantial findings on the Mangyan script was Dr. Schadenberg whom Blumentritt acknowledged as the one "who has been able to give us the first linguistic samples of one of the Mangyan idioms." Schadenberg himself went through the island of Mindoro around 1890 and discovered that the Mangyans did not only have their own alphabet but also used it in written communication. In his own particular way, Blumentritt noted, Dr. Schadenberg

> ...went about gathering sample (proofs) of his discovery in which activity the governor of the island, Don Maximo Lillo, and Don Ramon Valencia, secretary of the provincial council and officer of great service to the ethnology of the Philippines zealously helped him. Thus he succeeded in bringing together seven bamboo pieces with inscribed script signs. For some of them, Schadenberg received also keys and translations.⁶⁰

Although it was then generally supposed that the Mangyans were nomadic people, Jordana's account not only negated this view but provided an intriguing point of comparison with that of the Christian *indio* habitations. Jordana, in effect, emphasizes that

> Almost everyone has huts; only very few wander about in the mountains, without any particular place of residence. These huts are small and miserable and generally are made from bamboo and bejuco. The way they are built corresponds completely to that common among the Christian indios. Their household belongings are composed of some pots, a kind of frying pan, mats, and luxury items which they got in commerce with the Christian indios only at a high price.⁶¹

The natural simplicity of the Mangyans, coupled with honesty and conscientiousness in keeping promises, made them, according to Jordana, easy prey to lowland exploitation. The Hispanized Indios, he continues,

⁵⁷ *Ibid., loc. cit.*
⁵⁸ *Ibid., loc. cit.*
⁵⁹ *Ibid., loc. cit.*
⁶⁰ *Ibid., loc. cit.*
⁶¹ Ferdinand Blumentritt, "Die Mangianen der Insel Mindoro," *op. cit.*, p. 217.

> ...exploits them to their heart's desire by making them work heavily in the ricefields or using them to cut and carry trees and this only for a handful of rice. Also in commercial relations they have to suffer from the effects of the greed of the Christians, receiving only worthless objects in exchange for enormous quantities of wax bejuco and other things. *This abuse has already become an extreme scandal, since aside from the commercial trickeries, slavery still exists and still is in practice among the Christian indios* (italics mine—V.B.L.).[62]

What Jordana refers to as "slavery" is defined in terms of economic dependency rooted in the *pautangan* system between lowlanders and Mangyans. In this system, the lowlanders generally

> ...give the Manguianes an advance of palay, a thing or other objects for which they do not at once like to get the payment but instead expect that the Mangyans should give back their debts through work in their fields. This apparently legal contract transforms the Mangyans into a true slave, since the landowner gives a very low value to the work and besides adds interest to the debt which has not yet been paid through work; when a new necessity forces them to make another debt, the same is done earlier so that the debt made by the Mangyans, instead of decreasing, increases enormously and he sees himself forced to work during his entire life for the small sum which he first received.[63]

While lowland exploitation of Mangyans did exist in the Spanish era, it should not be dissociated from the chain of exploitation which linked it up to world commerce. The lowlanders, themselves subject to the abuse of Spaniards, set the chain of exploitation within Philippine society, quite unknown in the pre-Spanish era.

The oppressive system of Spanish control may have driven many Mangyan groups into the interior, but there were some who remained within the sphere of Spanish control. In such cases, the Mangyans were indirectly ruled by the Spaniards through the *commisario de Manguianes,* an official chosen from a neighboring Christian pueblo or *rancheria* and who then had to function as an intermediary in all official meetings and other occasions. In turn, each Mangyan tribe or rancheria had a chief who, through election or general agreement, acquired this honor and was accorded all the respect due a person of authority. Those Mangyans who lived very closely to the Christian settlements generally asked the provincial governor to confirm the authority of their heads through a piece of document. Jordana is

[62] *Ibid.*
[63] *Ibid.,* p. 218.

careful to note, however, that this practice was completely unknown in the rancherias of the interior.

In matters "moral" and "legal," the Mangyans are shown by Jordana to be more conscientious than their lowland brothers. He notes that the legal customs of the Manguianes

> ... are very strict. Adultery is punished with death in the same way that they also have very harsh punishment for robbery; however, they are not used with extreme strictness among some tribes. In general one can say that the customs of the Manguianes have a good basis of legality and morality. They fulfill conscientiously their promises, they do not deceive nor cheat, on the contrary these very high qualities combined with their natural naivete make them victims of the Christian indios.[64]

Speaking of morals and ethics, the Mangyans could not be rightfully deemed "more backward" than their "Hispanized" lowland kins. In point of fact, almost all the Spanish accounts of these people noticeably present them as honest, upright, and trustworthy beings. Yet, faced with opportunists, such high moral attributes became more of a liability than an asset. Jordana again observes that one

> ... cannot help admiring the submissiveness and patience of the Mangyan who submits himself with resignation to this hateful exactions. Even if flight into the thickness of the forest could be sufficient to save him since it can be said with complete certainty that no Christian indio would dare enter it, and take him back from his hiding place.[65]

The Mangyans were not without awareness of a Supreme Being. They also believed in the immortality of the soul, even though only in a vague way, and this found expression, Jordana explains, "neither in religious custom nor in whatever ceremonies." The almost monotheistic concept of God, however, was adulterated by their fear of spirits, expressed in their belief that the souls of the dead do not leave the place where they lived during their lifetime. Consequently,

> ... they believe themselves always surrounded by the spirits of their fathers, grandfathers, and ancestors by whom they are protected and defended in times of danger and by whom they are punished if they are bad or they act in a bad way.[66]

The lighter side of Mangyan life consisted of occasional dancing and singing, possibly held on special occasions, as the marriage of a

---

[64] *Ibid.*, p. 217.
[65] *Ibid.*, p. 218.
[66] *Ibid.*

couple. Presumably unaware of the other Mangyan musical instruments, Jordana identified only one which he compared to the Chinese violin—one having two strings.[67] Their songs and melodies, relates Jordana, did not differ markedly from those of the Christian indios, since, in order to ask for rain from their supreme being, "they sing a chant which in some places is called *malaguia."* Marriage itself was a special activity participated in by the whole family. It was always preceded

> ... by a getting together and agreement of the families of both parties. In the ceremony, these two families gather together and the parents or the nearest relatives take hold of a pot or any other breakable object which they consequently throw to the ground so that the marriage would be unbreakable.
>
> By some tubus, the following custom follows this ceremony: bride and groom lie down in each one of a particular hammock after which the respective parents swing their child up to the moment when, upon the nearing of both hammocks, the man leaps into the hammock of the woman which ends the entire thing. After this, a feast is held which consists of a meal, songs, and dances.[68]

From the point of contact with Spain in 1570 up to the end of Spanish rule, the natives of Mindoro went through tumultuous periods in their history. Confronted with an overwhelming colonial force that sought to subjugate and turn them into vassals and converts, the people could not but change. Pressures thus inevitably brought about responses. The sources that were examined in this chapter appear to allow the inference that the Mangyans may have constituted themselves as relatively distinct groups as a result of these pressures from the outside.

---

[67] Possibly the *git-git*, whose strings are made out of human hair.
[68] *Ibid., loc. cit.*

PART II

CONTACTS AND PRESSURES IN THE 20TH CENTURY

THE end of the Spanish regime, which otherwise marked the beginning of a new era, did not in any way stop the degradation of the island of Mindoro. At the close of the 19th century, it was celebrated primarily for "the unsavory reputation of its people, the heaviness of its rainfall, and the deadliness of the miasma in its fever-smitten lowlands."[1] In no way does the description reflect an island of major importance which Mindoro was in the past.

With the coming of the Americans, the interior inhabitants of Mindoro were brought increasingly into contact with the outside world. While diverse Mangyan groupings had become known in the Spanish period, more intensive knowledge of these people was gathered during the American period and the years that followed. Such knowledge, however, initially came from naturalistic studies that treated the Mangyans as no more than curio objects and subjects for exhibit purposes. It was along this line that some Mangyans and representatives of other "savage" ethnic groups were sent to the St. Louis exposition in the United States in 1904 as part of the exhibits.

Notwithstanding this unwholesome view of the non-Christian tribes, a number of American field researchers brought to the fore through their zeal a better knowledge of ethnic differentiation of the Mangyans. More ethnographic and linguistic areas were covered by them—though, of course, a significant number of Mangyans remained cut off from the mainstream of an evolving national life.

The concept of a "minority" became increasingly manifest as Americans worked out a policy of isolation rather than admixture of the lowland and highland peoples—i.e., the Christian and non-Christian groups. The idea of "non-Christian" tribes, fostered by the creation of special government rules for them and by efforts to restructure them into Indian-like reservations, all the more enhanced their position as a group distinct from what the Americans considered socio-politically as "Filipinos." In apparent response to this conservative concept, an antithetical idea emerged—that of "integration." This sprang from the concept of nationality which became a more domi-

---

[1] Dean C. Worcester, *The Philippine Islands and their People* (New York: The MacMillan Co., 1899), p. 362.

nant force from the Commonwealth period onwards, as the ideals which brought forth the Filipino nation late in the 19th century acquired more urgency and relevance, with the approach and then final attainment of independence.

This second part thus takes into account the diverse acculturative pressures that impinged on the lives of the Mangyans at the close of the 19th century up to the post-colonial era. An attempt is made to cover all existing literature relevant to the problem, and to check how old and new lowland forces alike have shaped present majority-minority relations in Mindoro.

Though the term "Mangyan" has a long history of usage, it was only in this century that the people known by this name became more accurately identified. Starting with naturalistic studies carried out by Worcester and moving progressively on to more scientific studies pioneered by Gardner, followed by Schebesta, further developed by Conklin, and augmented by contemporary researchers like Tweddel, Postma, Iturralde, Kikuchi, the MacDonalds, Pennoyer and others— knowledge of the diverse Mangyan groups today bears greater accuracy and substance than was previously the case.

Based on the existing studies and this writer's own research, it is clear that the term "Mangyan" refers to as many as six different groups scattered from the northern to the southernmost tip of Mindoro. Generally, they are classified into two major groups: the northern and southern groups speaking related languages. The northern group includes the *Iraya, Alangan,* and the *Tadyawan,* while the *Hanunoo,* the *Buhid* and the *Tawbuid* are classified "southern." The "Ratagnons", traditionally included among the "Mangyans", have been proven by Tweddel to be non-indigenous to Mindoro since they speak *Cuyonon,* a Visayan dialect. In truth, the Ratagnons today may be considered "extinct," in the sense that they no longer constitute a discernible ethnic type in Mindoro.

How We Perceive the Mangyans Today. At the turn of the century, however, the various Mangyan groups were still considered as a totality in relation to the coastal Christian groups. Thus, through more than seven decades, their relation to the total Filipino community was conceived in different ways by policy-makers of varying hues and views. These policies ranged from "isolation" in the early part of the American colonial regime to that of "integration" rooted in the concept of nationality which became a more dominant force from the Commonwealth era on.

Manifold pressures impinged upon the lives of the Mangyans as they related to the outside world of the 20th century. Old pressures were intensified during the American colonial era and even under the Philippine Republic. Pressures on land, properties and even life, constituted the revitalized forces that encroached on Mangyan life. Generally, these pressures came from land-hungry migrants whose number increased considerably over several decades. On the other hand, the intensification of government programs directly affecting the minorities brought agents into the interior who, instead of helping in the Mangyan development program, further contributed to the growing malaise among these people.

The combined economic, social, governmental, and religious pressures evoked varied responses from the beleaguered Mangyans. In a way, their varying reactions to these pressures were contributory to their being distinguished from one another. The relative isolation of the Hanunoo for several decades helped them preserve their basic culture, whereas the undirected association of the Iraya with the lowlanders contributed to their partial assimilation into lowland Tagalog culture. These varied responses of the ethnic groups themselves seem to furnish the beginnings of an answer to the problem of integrating them within the total national culture.

Chapter Three

Perception and Reality
of Mangyan Diversity

THE American era ushered in renewed interest in explorations as well as in the study of tribal peoples in the hinterlands of the Philippines. In Mindoro, such explorations initially took the form of naturalistic cum reconnaissance trips, like those undertaken by Dean C. Worcester. This pioneering American researcher visited Mindoro and other major islands in 1887 and 1890 and published his first work on the peoples of the Philippines in 1899. Worcester's study, however, merely gave a vague sketch of the varying ethnic groups as he was motivated by forces quite alien to the genuine desire for research. Significantly, the "explorer" became the Secretary of the Interior and member of the powerful Philippine Commission shortly after the establishment of American rule in the country.

More obsessed with the capture of the elusive *tamaraw* than with the thorough study of the Mangyans, Worcester confined his ethnographic research only to the groups he encountered along the historic Baco river—a place generally described today as the home of the Iraya-Alangan people. His reference to the use of coiled rattan skirt as well as to the use of bark-cloth[1] and the nomadic life of the tribe matches later accounts on the Iraya-Alangan group of Northern Min-

---

[1] The writer herself encountered in a recent field trip to Baco, Oriental Mindoro, one Alangan woman wearing the same attire—a number of rattan cords coiled around her waist and hips, showing persistence of traditional forms of clothing.

doro. Worcester, however, simply identified the group as "Mangyans." His account depicts a primitive group without permanent shelter, whose members

> ...wander through the woods by day, sleeping wherever night overtakes them, with no other roof than they can extemporize by binding a few rattan or palm leaves together and throwing them over a framework of poles or sticking their butts into the grounds so as to give them a slight inclination...Their only utensils were a few earthen pots; their only weapons, crude iron machetes.[2]

Despite this apparent lack of cohesion and organization among the Baco Mangyans, they had definite ways of transmitting messages among themselves. Worcester noted the practice of striking a particularly large tree with a big club to communicate to others over a broad distance. Describing further his encounter with them, Worcester expressed the common and condescending view that the tribal peoples were childlike in nature:

> Here then were the dreaded headhunters and cannibals, of whom we had heard such alarming reports. We kept a sharp eye on them at first but our precautions were entirely needless. They were as harmless as children. They were far more afraid of us than we were of them, but after we had won their confidence they furnished us endless amusement.[3]

A number of other studies concerning the Mangyans were also undertaken during this period, but, like Worcester's, these consisted mostly of short-term visits and explorations. In addition, they discussed other subjects and did not concentrate solely on the Mangyans, being general surveys of savage or exotic peoples. An example is A. Henry Savage Landor's work, which covers a whole range of tribal peoples from the northern to the southern Philippines.[4] Most works of this nature provided very general descriptions, often only playing up features in the native culture to project the desired primitiveness.

One of the first Mangyan researchers to set a new trend of study by ending the tendency to rely on short visits and explorations was Fletcher Gardner. A U.S. Army contract surgeon stationed at Bulalacao, Mindoro, Gardner lifted the study of the Mangyans to a

---

[2] Dean C. Worcester, *The Philippine Islands and Their People* (New York: The MacMillan Co., 1899), p. 362.
[3] *Ibid.*
[4] *The Gems of the East, Sixteen Thousand Miles of Research Travel Among Wild and Tame Tribes of Enchanting Islands* (New York and London: Harpers and Brothers, 1904).

higher plane with his extensive research on the language, script, culture and traditions of the group he identified as "Hampangan." His numerous field trips in the interior likewise brought him in touch with a number of other groups, resulting in more authoritative accounts of the Mangyans. Unlike earlier researchers, Gardner relied more heavily on empirical observations than on mere hearsay gleaned from prejudiced lowlanders.

Gardner identified the "Hampangan" as a group occupying an ill-defined area ranging from a point somewhere toward the interior of Mangarin on the south coast to Bongabong on the east coast.[5] He described them as

> ...pure Malay, of rather small stature, of rather light color, often plump, well-formed, and by Malay standards good-looking. The hair is usually straight, rarely wavy, and never curly or kinky. The teeth are usually black and worn, from constant use of betel-nut without cleansing... they tattoo the body.[6]

Compared with present-day accounts, Gardner's descriptions of the Hampangan, whose name according to him, meant "they who are awaited,"[7] parallel those usually given of the Hanunoo Mangyans. It is in fact quite safe to conclude that the Hampangans and the Hanunoo are one and the same people. While other writers consider Gardner's appelation as erroneous,[8] the name Hanunoo itself is a misnomer since it is only an adjective used by this particular group to underscore its authenticity in relation to "other Mangyans"—the Hanunoo being in a word, "the true Mangyans." Be that as it may, the group described in Gardner's account presents a culture relatively more structured and sophisticated than the other Mangyan groups iden-

---

[5] Fletcher Gardner, "The Hampangan Mangyans of Mindoro," original manuscript (Frt. Crook, Nebraska: Jan. 12, 1906), p. 1 in *Mindoro-Palawan Paper No. 1, Beyer Collection. Philippine Ethnography—A Collection of Original Sources.* (Cambridge: Harvard University microreproduction). Henceforth referred to in this work as M-P Papers.

[6] *Ibid.*

[7] Gardner's informants were two "Hampangan" women. It is interesting to note that, among the pioneer Mangyan researchers and even including those of contemporary times, only Gardner seems to have used the term "Hampangan." See "Letters Relating to the Mangyans of Mindoro," (Bulalacao, Mindoro: June 15, 1904), M-P Paper No. 4, p. 1.

[8] Cf., for instance, Encarnacion Iturralde, "The Religion of the Mangyans of Mindoro: An Anthropological Approach to Mission Work," Ph.D. dissertation (University of Sto. Tomas Graduate School, Manila: June, 1973), p. 101.

tified in this period. As the pioneer ethnographer of the Mangyans observed:

> The principal industry is agriculture, which consists of growing upland rice, camotes, gabi, chili, squashes, and the like, on buras (?) in the woods... The houses attached to these clearings are often well-built, with buri-thatched sides and roof, and have frequently several rooms built as separate houses around a central platform... As new ground is usually put under cultivation nearly every year, the house may remain for a long time, provided there may be no deaths in the family.[9]

Gardner's study showed substantially not only the intricate way the Hampangans adorned themselves but likewise their metal work, basketry and weaving. It noted nonetheless that they did not make mats nor pots. These products were procured from the coastal natives or "from a rancheria of Bukid Mangyans, who are subject to a chief called Gihitän, who himself is a Hampangan."[10]

Whether or not there was marked social stratification among the Hampangan or the other Mangyan groups is not clear from Gardner's account nor any other written in the same period. He only makes reference to the Mangyans of a certain district who acknowledged a chief or headman assuming various roles. Such a man, according to him,

> ... settles their disputes, protects them from injustices and... they owe (him) a portion of their labor and all their obediences. They are always subject to the headman's call. If he calls them for a hunt, they come; and at his suggestions, they make their caingins, harvest the crop which they use in common...[11]

Gardner is quick to note, however, that the authority of the headman was not absolute, the Mangyans having considerable freedom among themselves. Among the Hampangans, he points out that the "chiefship... is not hereditary."[12] The powers of their chief were limited and disputes were settled by a council of the old men of the same or neighboring rancherias.

In addition to his study of the Hampangan morals and religion, Gardner covered at length the Hampangan syllabary and *ambahan* poetry. His work probably constitutes one of the first published ac-

---

[9] Gardner, "The Hampangan," p. 5.
[10] *Ibid.*, p. 6.
[11] Fletcher Gardner, "The Mangyans," M-P Paper No. 2, p. 26.
[12] Gardner, "The Hampangan," *op. cit.*, p. 6.

counts of the Hampangan script and songs, including a considerable Hampangan word list. The songs he collected and translated himself throw some light on the philosophy of life of a very amiable people.[13]

Continued research and frequent visits to Mangyan settlements provided Gardner with greater insight as to the diversity of these people. The use of Mangyan informants, like one literate woman named Luyon, led to a more distinct ethnic classification of the Mangyans. To him, there were

> ...four classes of Mangyans... Ratagnon, Hanono-o, Bukid and Bangon. Those from Bulalacao to Mangarin mixed with the Bisaya are called Ratagnons. Those who go from Bongabon to here (Manaul) are Hanono-os. The Bukid Mangyans are far from town and do not visit it. The Bangon (forest) Mangyans are farther still and are without woven cloth; the bark of a tree is their clothing (sic). Different is the Ratagnon speech, different the Hanono-o dialect, different the Bukid language, different the Bangon tongue.[14]

A letter dated September 27, 1904 addressed by Gardner to Dr. Merton Miller, then acting chief of the Ethnological Survey, gives us a glimpse of Gardner's idea of research and his genuine interest in the Mangyans. In it, he reports that

> ...I have asked them if they would like to have an Amercian (sic) who should look after their interests, in common with the other Mangyans of the Island, and they would greatly like to have it done. It would serve to make the protecting power of the government visible to them, as well as the coast natives, their oppressors. Is it not possible that something could be done by your department in that way? I am greatly interested in them both scientifically and humanly, and would be willing to resign my present position to accept it if I could secure an equal financial return. The idea is given for what it is worth. Whoever undertakes it should be well regarded by them, and should be able to live among them for extended periods, and to converse with them in their own language, or in Tagalog which most of them understand.[15]

As more scientifically-oriented men like Gardner engaged in the study of the Mangyans and as the means for data gathering acquired more refinement, specific aspects of the Mangyan culture became

---

[13] Cf. Appendix A.

[14] From the bamboo writing of Luyon cited in Fletcher Gardner and Ildefonso Maliwanag, *Indic Writings of Mindoro-Palawan Axis*, Bulletin No. 1, (San Antonio, Texas: Witte Memorial Museum, 1939), p. 68.

[15] From the collection of "Letters Relating to the Mangyans of Mindoro," M-P Paper No. 3, pp. 6-7.

known, ranging from "medical materials of a Mangyan mediquillo"[16] to the specific Mangyan languages and dialects.[17]

Contributions to the knowledge about the Mangyans came not only from American scholars but also from those of other nationalities, notably the German anthropologist Paul Schebesta. Denying the common allegation that some Mangyans originated from the Negritos, Schebesta affirmed that

> ...The Mangyans are not at all negritos: however, they are untouched by civilization and in many ways more primitive than these. For my trip to the Mangyans, I was impelled less by (an awareness of) the presence of negrito elements among them, but much more because of the wavy hair element (among them) similar to that of the Senoi of Malaya. I wanted to be sure of this...[18]

While most writers classified the Mangyans according to their geographical location, Schebesta grouped them according to salient points in their culture—that is, he grouped them into "primitive" or "civilized", "savage" or "domesticated." Based on this, he came up with two major groupings: the northern "savage" and the southern "domesticated" groups. Schebesta theorized that the great disparity between the northern and southern Mangyan cultures might have resulted from the intermingling of "Moros" with the "southern" Mangyans who, as a result, "took on higher culture forms and habits." He further observed that "these southern Mangyans are usually easier to approach and cannot be compared with the primitive Mangyans of the north."[19]

The Second World War brought a momentary end to the increasing number of specialized studies on the non-Christian tribes of Mindoro. Among the first to resume field work after the war and the first to live among the Hanunoo for an extended period of time was Harold C. Conklin, who has probably published the most literature on this ethnic group. Unlike his predecessors, Conklin was unaccom-

---

[16] Cf. Harley M. Bartlett's "The geographic distribution, migration, and dialectal mutation of certain plant names in the Philippines and Netherlands India, with special reference to the materials of a Mangyan mediquillo," *Proceedings of the Sixth Pacific Science Congress of the Pacific Science Association*, Berkeley and Los Angeles, 6 (4), 1940; pp. 85-110.

[17] An early form of linguistic analysis of the Mangyan script is Edwin Emil Schneider's "Notes of the Mangyan Language," *Philippine Journal of Science* (1912) 7 (3, Sec. D): 157-88.

[18] Paul Schebesta, *Menschen Ohne Geschichte* (St. Gabriel-Modling, 1935), p. 134, as translated by Dr. Zeus Salazar.

[19] *Ibid.*

panied and initially financed the work himself. He has made substantial contributions to the knowledge about the Mangyans through his extensive studies on Mangyan culture, language and physical types. With the aid of modern methods and research techniques, he obtained more reliable data on the different facets of Hanunoo life, even, for example, betel-chewing as this relates to beliefs and custom laws, aside from the Mangyan type of shifting cultivation, their bamboo literacy, music, color categories as well as, in a more detailed way, the relation of Hanunoo culture to the plant world.[20] With Conklin, the study of the Hanunoo people reached a height never before attained by other researchers. His residence in the interior among the Hanunoo Mangyans themselves brought him into dynamic contact with them and gave him a full view of every facet of the life of a people never fully known previously by the outside world. Ethnic identification in Mindoro did in fact become definite with his reports.

In his preliminary report on his field work in 1949, Conklin enumerated nine main ethnographic groups, each speaking a separate language: the Iraya, Alangan, Nauhan, Bukid, Hanunoo, Ratagnon, Batangan and Bangon.[21] A continuing study of the Mangyans gave Conklin a more comprehensive view of the people, resulting in an even more distinct classification of the different ethnic groups. When Conklin thus wrote his dissertation on ethno-botany seven years later he listed eight major groupings, dropping Nauhan from the earlier list.[22]

Concerning ethnic types in Mindoro, Conklin observed evidence of limited interbreeding among some of the ethnic groups and between

---

[20] Cf. Harold C. Conklin, "Betel Chewing Among the Hanunoo," Abstract No. 66, *Fourth Far-Eastern Pre-history Congress*. It shows among other things, how the use of betel among the Hanunoo is closely interwoven with much of their core culture. The article can also be found in: *Philippine Heritage: The Making of a Nation*, ed. Alfredo R. Roces (1974), pp. 175-79. Cf. likewise, "Maling, A Hanunoo Girl from the Philippines" reprint from *In the Company of Man — Twenty Portraits by Anthropologists*, ed. Joseph B. Casagrande (Harper: New York, 1960), pp. 102-25. This contains a graphic illustration of the life of a Hanunoo girl—her daily mode of living, transition from childhood to maturity. Also, "Hanonoo Agriculture: A Report on an Integrated System of Shifting Cultivation in the Philippines," *FAO Forestry Development Paper No. 12* (Rome, 1957).

[21] Harold C. Conklin, "Preliminary Report on Field Work—On the Islands of Mindoro and Palawan, Philippines," *American Anthropologist*, Vol. 51, No. 2, p. 268.

[22] Harold C. Conklin, "The Relation of Hanunoo Culture to the Plant World," unpublished Ph.D. dissertation, Yale University, p. 44.

these and recent arrivals along the coast. In his view, none of the groups is unmixed but they apparently represent three different clusters of physical characteristics. It may thus be possible to trace racial origins to other areas. In an anthropometric inquiry into Mindoro racial defines, Leo Estel recognized the importance of Conklin's findings, convinced that the study of the Iraya, Nauhan and Hanunoo "should throw some new light on racial movements in northern Indonesia."[23]

Until the establishment of the Philippine Republic, Filipino contribution to the accumulating knowledge concerning the Mangyans was confined to sketchy magazine articles and reports. It must be pointed out, however, that the informants of all earlier scholars, particularly those who could not go into the interior themselves, were Filipinos. The process of data-gathering and field work was nevertheless left to Western scholars in general. One of the first Filipino scholars to break this monopoly was Marcelino Maceda who himself went into the interior for two months, and supplemented this by two other short visits. His work complemented what had been known till then about the Mangyans, as its focus was on the northern ethnic groups which had been left out by previous researchers, including Conklin. While the studies of the southern group had been invariably thorough, several facets of the northern Mangyan socio-cultural life were yet unexplored. Maceda filled this gap with the considerable amount of data gathered during his field study.

Writing on the age-old problem of finding an appropriate term to identify the diverse ethnic groups in Mindoro, Maceda posited that:

> The question concerning the name of these aboriginal inhabitants of Oriental Mindoro could be very well settled by these people themselves. In all the places visited by the writer, he has always asked them their real name as population group. The answer to the question put up was uniform: They told him that 'they are Mangyans.' The variations may then be ascribed to the fact that they, the Mangyans, always refer to the places where they live, and hence this writer supposes that the former researchers have taken the names of these places for their tribal "designations."[24]

[23] Leo Arthur Estel, *Mindoro Anthropometry and Racial Origins in Northern Indonesia* (Berkeley: University of California, 1950), Ph.D. dissertation, p. 5.
[24] Marcelino N. Maceda, "A Brief Report on Some Mangyans of Northern Oriental Mindoro," *Unitas,* 40(1): 102-55.

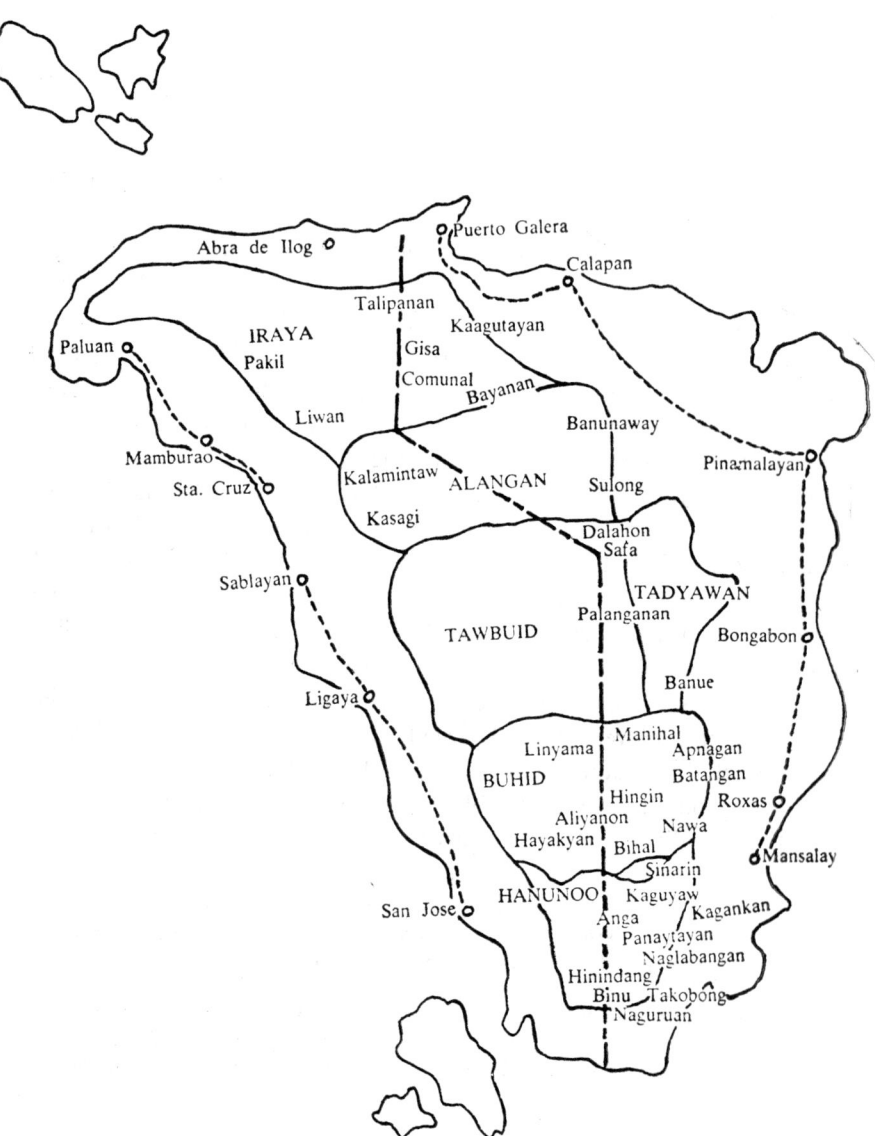

Present distribution of the different Mangyan tribes in Mindoro.

Maceda's statement seems to be reflected in Schebesta's own account of some northern Mangyans who, when queried about their tribal designations, gave, apart from the term "coastal Mangyans," three other groups whose names were based on geographical location: *taga-ulunan, taga-gaba* and *taga-langan*.[25]

The '50s saw the mushrooming of studies on the Mangyans for varied reasons. On July 4, 1950, a team of Protestant Missionaries eager to make a breakthrough among the mountain tribes hitherto unreached by intensive evangelization embarked upon a new program of language study and gospel recordings in the different Mangyan dialects as a prelude to mission work among them. In truth, specific studies on the different Mangyan dialects in this period were made primarily by zealous missionaries eager to spread the gospel.[26]

The eagerness of the evangelical workers to reach all the different Mangyan groups set a new trend in Mangyan studies, the specialized study of languages other than the Hanunoo. As the groups speaking these languages did not possess a material culture interesting enough for researchers, they were generally overlooked. Through the efforts of the missionaries, detailed knowledge of the dialects and cultures of the Iraya, Buhid and other groups became available.

During the postwar era, therefore, Mangyan studies became more specialized and scientific in perspective. Working for his doctoral dissertation in 1957, Leon Estel studied Mindoro anthropometry and racial origins at length, coming out with conclusions which further gave light to the cultural roots of the Mangyans. Thus, information concerning Mangyan racial types became more definite. Estel's conclusion was that:

> The data presented show three groups on Mindoro. The Iraya are phenotypically Veddoids, the Nauhan an aberrant Mongoloid group, and the Hanunoo one of the early Asiatic types. The Negritoes, supposed to

[25] Schebesta, *op. cit.*, p. 139. "Taga-ulunan" may well refer to the Bukids or "those who live higher up the mountains" (from the word *ulunan*, the place of the *ulun* or "source," cf. Tag. *ulu*, "head," Malay *hulu*, "head"; "headwaters" Bikol *ulunan* "pillow," headrest); *taga-langan* are literally those "from the east"— the Irayas, and *Taga-gaba* or *ibaba* refers to the ones described as in constant touch with the Tagalogs.
[26] Cf. for instance Marie R. Barham, "The Phonemes of the Buhid (Mangyan) Language of Eastern Mindoro." *Oceania Linguistic Monographs*, Capell and Wurm, eds. (1955); 3:4-9, and Frances H. Williamson, "Translators at Work," *The Millions* 80 (6-June), 1954. Miss Hazel Page also did an intensive study of the Iraya language, which served as a major source for Tweddel's study cited elsewhere in this book.

be the inhabitants of Indonesia, form no discernible element in the population of Mindoro. The Southern Mongoloids are only represented by a coastal fringe of recent settlers. Why this should be is not readily apparent...[27]

Estel also asserted that comparisons of the Iraya with other racial types revealed closer affinity with the Toalas on the island of Celebes and the Sakai of Malay Peninsula, which are all remnants of Veddoid populations once found in a wide area extending from India, across Indonesia, and possibly to Australia. Though the Iraya are not "unmixed," they are in his view among the best representatives yet recorded of the short, curly-haired, dark-skinned "Veddoids."

Working on linguistic similitude as a basis for ethnic groupings, Colin E. Tweddel, who specialized on the Iraya Mangyan language, came out with two major types: the northern and the southern groups, each speaking related languages. Following his criteria for classification, the Iraya, Alangan and the Tadyawan constitute the northern group, while the Hanunoo, the Buhid and the Batangan form the southern.[28] Unlike previous researchers, Tweddel omitted the Ratagnon from the list as he is of the opinion that, though deemed "Mangyan," they are not really indigenous to Mindoro, since they speak Cuyonon, a Visayan dialect used in Cuyo and Semirara islands as well as Palawan. The missionary-linguist attributed the confusing assignment of tribal names to the cross mountain spread and the relative isolation of peoples in mountain pockets.

Iturralde, on the other hand, asserted that much of the initial confusion regarding the Mangyans was "really due to the indiscriminate giving of one generic name to all the various ethnic groups of Mindoro."[29] In this, she merely echoes Conklin who himself criticized the term "Mangyan" as being too general for use in a tribal sense. He avers that it cannot be put on the same level as other terms denoting specific groupings, such as Tagalog, Kankanai, Tausog, etc. In some of the Mindoro non-Christian names, he explains, "Mangyans"

---

[27] Estel, *op. cit.*, p. 15.
[28] Colin E. Tweddel, "The Identity and Distribution of the Mangyan Tribes of Mindoro, Philippines," *Anthropological Linguistics*, 12(6): 189. Mary Bongco, one of the leaders of an enterprising group of Christian laymen undertaking a four-year Mangyan Integrated Development Program, says that the term *Batangan* being just the name of a large river near the settlement of these people, should not be confused with the *Batangan,* one of the names used to refer to the Tawbuids.
[29] Iturralde, *op. cit.*, p. 92.

... means *man* or *person* (as in Alangan); in some it means their specific linguistic group as differentiated from others (as in Iraya, and sometimes in Hanunoo) and in others, it signifies a group other than the speaker's own (as in Buhid). In the Christian and pagan languages in which it occurs, Mangyan is an unanalyzable base ... The word "Mangyan" in fact is often used locally as a synonym for "servant," "debt slave" and other status terms of that class.[30]

While researchers recognize the inadequacy of the term "Mangyan" to refer to the minority groups in Mindoro, its use prevails even today simply because a more appropriate term does not exist. However, if the fact that these people share the same historical experience is to serve as a basis for the appelation, the continued use of the term "Mangyan" is reasonable. As the essence of words changes in time, the use of the name "Mangyan" today to refer to the totality of minority groups living in the interior of Mindoro is indeed tenable.

Among the Catholic missionaries, Antoon Postma has contributed most toward the better understanding of Hanunoo culture. Better known today as the "Protector of the Mangyans," Postma transcends the usual missionary concern for conversions. He undertook an extensive study of the Hanunoo culture ending in a comprehensive collection of this people's literary and poetic expression. The knowledge of the *ambahan* today, as well as other aspects of the rich Hanunoo cultural heritage, is largely due to his painstaking efforts.[31]

While substantive knowledge of the Hanunoo Mangyans already exists today, information concerning the other groups still leaves much to be desired. An imbalance thus prevails in the study of the Mangyans. Owing to their proximity to the coastal region and their rich culture, the Hanunoo have always attracted researchers. Other groups living in squalor and relatively isolated in the interior remain relatively unknown to the outside world. A cursory look at the studies made thus far readily shows this imbalance. Of about eight major researches (seven master's theses and one dissertation) undertaken

---

[30] Harold C. Conklin, *The Relation of Hanunoo Culture to the Plant World*, op. cit., p. 75.

[31] Cf. Antoon Postma, *Treasure of a Minority*, Revised ed., (Manila: Arnoldus Press, 1972), 160 pp. Postma, however, insists on the use of the term "Mangyan" rather than "Hanunoo" to refer to this ethnic group. In fact, he strongly advocates that "Mangyan" be used singly to refer to this group.

by Filipino scholars, two deal in part with the Iraya and the rest concentrate on the Hanunoo people of Occidental Mindoro.[32]

Among researches conducted by other scholars, the interest did not vary much until recently, when a few enterprising anthropologists dared to make a breakthrough among those Mangyans still hidden in the depths of Mt. Halcon. In 1969, Yasushi Kikuchi undertook an exploratory study of the Batangans of Western Mindoro to examine the feasibility of making this group the basis for a doctoral dissertation. As defined in his preliminary report, the Japanese researcher was concerned with two specific problems: the emergence of an axial family line in relation to the family line of the leaders of the local group and the social mechanism for inheriting ritual paraphernalia and the succession to magical religious offices.[33]

Two years thereafter, a French couple undertook an ethnographic study of two further groups for around four months.[34] Charles MacDonald's report includes a brief account of the agriculture, hunting, fishing and knowledge of medicinal plants of the Iraya-Alangan people. The wife made a short study of the vocabulary used in the harvesting of honey. Unfortunately, the couple did not go farther into the interior but cut short their research before their objectives could be fully realized.

Of late, an American anthropologist explored the more inaccessible mountainous regions of Western Mindoro and undertook an intensive study of the Tawbuid. Guided by a converted Tawbuid Mang-

[32] Cf. Felix Almero, "Customs and Mores of the Mangyans of Occidental Mindoro," Far Eastern University, 1951; Fe Bobon, "The Hanunoo Mangyans in Panaytayan, Mansalay, Oriental Mindoro," University of Manila, 1970; Marcelino Calleja, "A Study of the Culture of the Mangyans of Mindoro," Lyceum University, Manila, 1960; P.E. Dimalibot, "Life and Culture of the Mangyans of Occidental Mindoro," National University, 1955; Mercedes A. Leviste, "The Role of Saclag Settlement School in the Uplift of the Lives of the Mangyans," University of Sto. Tomas, 1964; Emeterio de la Paz, "A Survey of the Hanunoo Mangyan Culture," University of Sto. Tomas, 1967; and Mila S. Tolentino, "Some Aspects of Iraya Mangyan Culture and their Implication for Education Programming," University of the East, 1969.

[33] Yasushi Kikushi, "Preliminary Consideration of the Social Structure of the Bayanan Group of the Batangan, Mindoro, Philippines," original manuscript, 16 pp.; also Seiichi Muratake and Yasushi Kikuchi, "Social Structure of the Batangan in Mindoro, Philippines," *SHA, A Quarterly Record of Social Anthropology*, Vol. 11, No. 2 (October 1968), pp. 30-61.

[34] Charles MacDonald, "Notes de terrain: Mindoro, Philippines" in *Langues Et Techniques Nature Et Société*, edité par Jacqueline M. C. Thomas and Lucien Bernot, Editions Klincksieck, (1971); Nicole Revel-MacDonald, "La collecte du miel," *Langues et Techniques: Nature et Société*, Editions Klincksieck, (1971).

yan, Douglas Pennoyer probed the hidden villages of this group generally identified as Batangans. As Kikuchi himself observed, the group commonly called Batangans, in spite of widespread similarities, have a number of sub-cultural and sub-social distinctions. The Tawbuids, according to Pennoyer, are relatively isolated and have no direct contact with lowlanders. Trade and exchange of goods are done through the Hanunoo people who serve as middlemen.[35] Undoubtedly, Pennoyer's work, when terminated, would constitute a pioneer study of this ethnic group.

Despite the relatively large number of studies here, there is still a dearth of studies concerning Mangyan groups other than the Hanunoo. Based on the trend of present studies, the Alangan, Tadyawans and Tawbuid groups need to be explored at length and constitute a real challenge to researchers interested in Mangyan studies. It cannot be denied, however, that we have acquired within the last seven decades or so a much deeper and more definite knowledge of at least the varied ethnic situation in Mindoro. This should be of great help not only in identifying the recent and continuing pressures on the various ethnic groups but likewise in understanding their context in terms of policy as formulated and implemented first by Americans, then by Filipinos in the Commonwealth and the Republic.

---

[35] Based on an interview with Mr. Douglas Pennoyer, July 1973, on the findings of his research among the Tawbuids. Mr. Pennoyer is presently connected with the Department of Anthropology, Washington State University.

Tamaraw Falls—one of Mindoro's many scenic spots. It is located between Puerto Galera and San Teodoro.

Fragments of a jar, porcelain wares and other vessels found in sites of indiscriminate diggings in barrios Minolo and Lumang-bayan, Mindoro.

A Ming blue-and-white plate inscribed with the characteristic Chinese script in the center, possibly 14th-15th century. Vessels like this are used by Buhid and Hanunoo Mangyans for sacrificial food offerings.

Jar with four dragons in high relief, possibly Yuan or early Ming (14th-15th century). Unearthed in Bo. Minolo, Puerto Galera.

Glazed black pottery with the incised Chinese character "tong" which means "equal." This type abounds in Naujan and Victoria burial sites.

THE "KUTKUTAN"

The "kutkutan" is the exhumation of the bones of a deceased Mangyan by his nearest relatives a year after his death, marking the end of the mourning period. Right photo shows his closest kin digging up the gravesite.

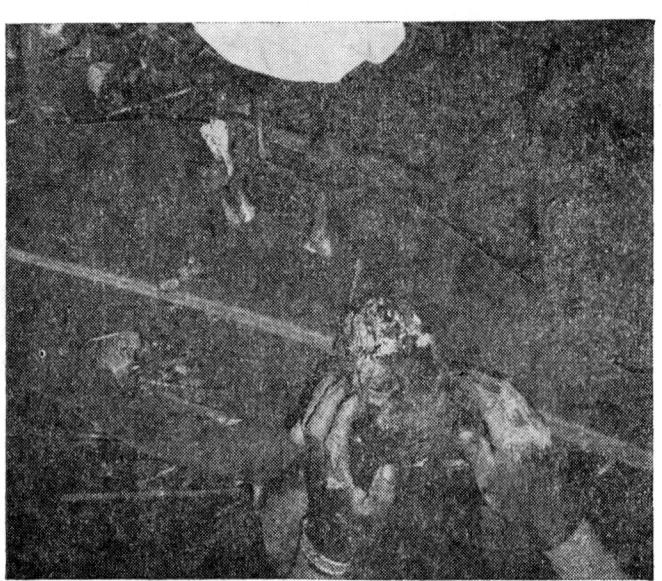

All the bones recovered from the grave are carefully sifted and gathered together.

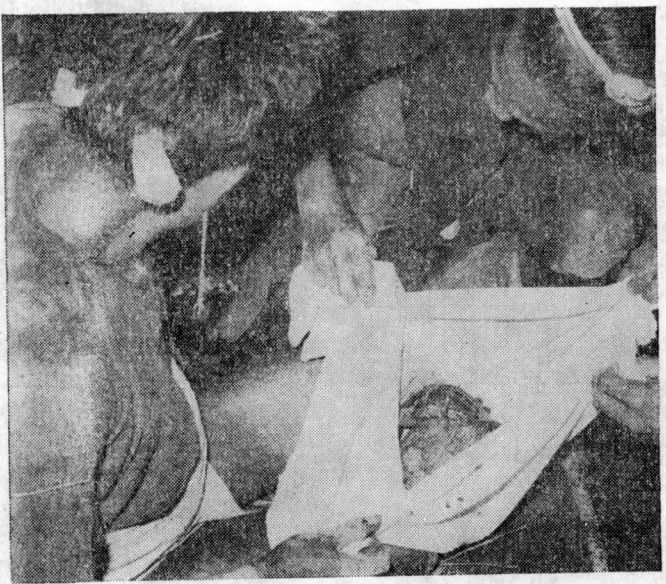

The bones are wrapped in two blankets placed on top of the other. Two ends of the blankets are tied up and these serve as the arms; the two other corners are knotted together to form the head.

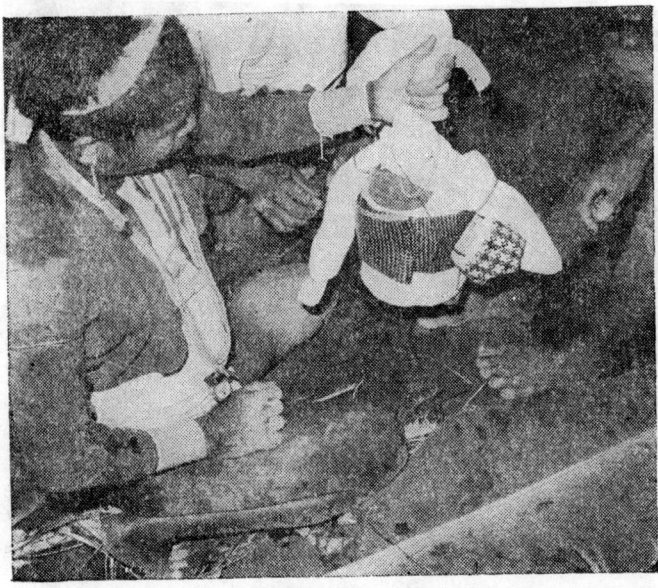

A relative of the deceased holds the knotted blankets containing the remains.

(*"Kutkutan"* photos by Jack Di-Benedetto)

The ruins of one of the earliest churches built in Mindoro can be found in Bancuro, Naujan.

Sign of innovation in an Iraya village—a small store adjacent to a newly-built nipa house.

An Iraya mother and daughter on their way to their kaingin.

An Alangan maiden wearing the classic nito-cord attire with tree bark toppings.

The Mangyans in session—a scene in the annual Mangyan Inter-"Tribal" Conference with the director of the Mangyan Integrated Development Program presiding.

Tawbuid Christianized folks pose for a picture after one of the Conference sessions.

Chapter Four

Pressures New
and Old

COUPLED with the presence of bandits or *tulisanes,* the already beleaguered inhabitants of Mindoro were further subjected to travail with the advent of America and its century. In 1902, a plague hit the island. The epidemic led to the death of numerous people and farm animals. It likewise resulted in scarcity of food, a situation heretofore unknown in the history of Mindoro.

However, despite the gloomy prospects for the new colonial masters, there were those among them that saw beyond the plague and the white men's tales of woe about the island and its inhabitants. The same year that the plague struck, Capt. Robert G. Offley, the first American civil governor in Mindoro, wrote to the "explorer turned Secretary of Interior," Dean C. Worcester, and observed that the island's primitive people were worthy of their concern:

> These people ... are, in my opinion, *a desirable acquisition and I shall do everything in my power to win them over* (Italics mine—V.B.L.) first by passing such laws as will protect them from the Filipino, who rob (sic) them on every occasion.[1]

This started a revitalized zeal for research and projects concerning the Mangyans, ending a few years later in the establishment of In-

---

[1] Excerpt from the letter to Dean C. Worcester, Secretary of Interior, by R. G. Offley, dated August 30, 1902, "Letters Relating to the Mangyans of Mindoro," M-P Paper No. 2, p. 1.

dian-like reservations and the San Jose sugar estate "where Mangyans were sent to work."

Projects of this sort would constitute a new type of pressure on the Mangyan groups. Other new ones would come with it as the century wore on, adding to the already old pressures which, to a certain extent, would intensify. These forms of pressures, old and new, are examined in this chapter with a view to identifying their effects on traditional Mangyan ways.

PRESSURES FROM AMERICAN ENTERPRISE

One of the first steps Worcester took as Secretary of the Interior was to secure display pieces from the Mangyans, while taking measures designed to win their confidence. An act passed on October 3, 1902, provides among other things, that some fifty pesos be used

> ... for materials suitable for distribution among the Manguianes of Mindoro, and that this be forwarded to the Governor of Mindoro with the request that he utilize it to please the Manguianes on the one hand, and on the other to secure by exchange, for the Philippine Museum, much needed specimens of Mindoro dress, arms, musical instruments, utensils, etc. ...[2]

Renewed efforts in gathering artifacts brought the American in closer touch with the Mangyans whose potential for labor and exploitation was laid bare to them. Not only were these people shy and withdrawn but also hardworking and honest. For Worcester and his associates, such traits were valuable assets for a contemplated sugar estate. Toward this end, purchase was made on October 4, 1904, of the San Jose estate, a friar land with a total area of 22,484.815 hectares.[3] In what seems to be more than just a coincidence, the Welch and Fairchild and Co., an American sugar enterprise, began to be interested at about the same period in buying lands for the proposed sugar central. Thus, when the San Jose Estate was purchased by the colonial government in 1904, a portion, covering an area of 334,872 sq. meters, was leased to one Eduard L. Poale, with the approval of Dean C. Worcester, acting in his capacity as Secretary of the Inte-

---

[2] Dean C. Worcester, "First Endorsement to Civil Government of the Philippines, Department of the Interior," official document dated October 3, 1903, M-P Paper No. 2, p. 5.
[3] Macario Z. Landicho, *The Mindoro Yearbook, 1901-1951* (Manila: Yearbook Publishers, 1952), p. 518.

rior.⁴ By virtue of this contract, the colonial government granted the lease to the Mindoro Sugar Company, subsidiary of Welch and Fairchild and Co. Through successive legislative acts, the company gained more power. One such act was passed by the Philippine Legislature in 1920 to give it authority "to own, control and cultivate certain land(s) situated in the province of Mindoro, lease and sell the land situated in the limit of the so-called San Jose Estate."⁵ Gardner referred to the notorious estate as a "place where Mangyans went to work." Thus, while claiming the role of "protector of the Mangyans," the Americans led by Worcester ingeniously carved themselves a niche in the existing chain of exploitation in Mindoro. In so doing, they constituted a new form of pressure clothed in the garb of "benevolence."

The situation did not escape the watchful eye of Filipino nationalists like Teodoro M. Kalaw and Lope K. Santos who bitterly and ingeniously denounced Worcester in an editorial which gave the name to the celebrated *Aves de Rapiña* case. The piece railed at the Americans' characteristic way of exploiting tribal people in the guise of "benevolence." It pointed out that:

> There are men who, besides being eagles, have the characteristics of the vulture, the owl and the vampire...
> Ascending the mountains of Benguet to classify and measure the skulls of the Igorots and study and civilize them and to spy in his flight with the eye of the bird of prey, where are the large deposits of gold, the prey concealed amidst the lonely mountains, to appropriate them to himself afterwards, thanks to legal facilities made and unmade at will, but always for his own benefit...
> Presenting himself on all occasions with the wrinkled brow of the scientist who consumes his life in the mysteries of the laboratory of sciences, when his whole scientific labor is confined to dissecting insects and importing fish eggs...
> Giving an admirable impulse to the discovery of wealthy lodes in Mindoro... and in other virgin regions of the archipelago with the money of the people; and under the pretext of the public good, when as a strict matter of truth, the object is to possess all the data and the key to the national wealth for his essentially personal benefits, as is shown *by the acquisition of immense properties registered under the names of others*...
> (Italics mine.—V.B.L.)⁶

⁴ *Ibid.*
⁵ *Ibid.*, p. 519.
⁶ "Reports of Cases determined in the Supreme Court of the Philippine Islands," *Philippine Reports*, Vol. 22 (Manila: Bureau of Printing, 1918), p. 47.

It is ironic but true that, while the writers of the editorial were found guilty of libel, Worcester himself figured two years later in a congressional investigation of charges akin to those mentioned in the exposé.[7] The investigation centered around the vast San Jose sugar estate which was surreptitiously run by him.

Worcester's interest in the Mangyans went beyond their recruitment as plantation workers. In 1904, he assembled an "exhibit" of various non-Christian peoples for the Lewis and Clark exposition in the United States. Six Mangyans were included in his "collection of savage peoples," but only five returned to Mindoro after six months for one died in America.[8]

The response of the Mangyans exposed to a world normally beyond their reach is vividly recorded in Gardner's account of the experience of one of these "exhibits," the young Macario:

> Macario and his father live at Pocanin. Macario was at St. Louis (i.e., exposition in the U.S.). Of course he is now somewhat (sic) among the Mangyans. He is a young chap with good sense. The visit helped him some too. His is the cleanest and best built house among them all... There is evidence, too, of this visit to the other world that must have seemed so like a dream to him. Macario used to show it himself whenever he came to town, before his civilized garb wore out. Since then he dresses a la Mangyan, but he was very proud of his clothes.
>
> His house built in the form of a "T," with the kitchen forming the stem and the two sleeping rooms the bar (?). One sleeping room is for the men and visitors when there chance to be any. The other is for the women of the house. But all dine together in the men's room. On the post of the one room were posted pictures of fine horses, some he had gathered at St. Louis... High up in another corner was a neat little souvenir cup with a mounted cane close beside it... A little pine box served as a cupboard, in which were some plates and spoons... these reminders of civilization seemed so incongruous among the dusky savages in a far away land. It was a chapter written large in the book called Life, where he who would read, might catch a glimpse of his own kind began. In a way, Macario, Sabong, Daliotan and Sanhogan (the Mangyans sent to the St. Louis Expo) had a vision. In a way, they felt but could not fathom the difference between the "Great City" and their own tropic

[7] See James H. Blount, *The American Occupation of the Philippines 1898-1912* (New York: G. P. Putman, 1912), p. 229.

[8] Merton Miller noted in his annual report for 1904 that at least one from each of the groups represented in the Exposition "died in St. Louis or on the way there," *Annual Reports of the War Department* (1904), Vol. 11, Part 2, (Washington: Government Printing Office, 1905), p. 422.

jungles. At best they might (they) sought to imitate which is about all the best (they) may do...⁹

Exposure to the outside world brings about a characteristic response—imitation. As some Mangyans were exposed to external influences, imitation brought about class consciousness, a realization that one can really "lord-it-all," given experience and knowledge beyond the reach of other tribal members. Imitation as a response thus brought elements alien if not anathema to the Mangyan socio-cultural system. This is best exemplified in the story of Sabong, which Gardner also recounts:

> "Sabong" is one of the Mangyans who saw the "great white City," and partly as a consequence of that fact, he has some queer ideas of justice. In Spanish times "Sabong" was a "cabeza de barangay"... Sometimes (sic) ago a girl decided to get married without asking Sabong anything about it which probably she ought not to have done according to the Mangyan custom. So when Sabong heard of the married (sic) he was very angry. Then he fined the girl's husband a bolo, a carabao, and nineteen pesos in money which was about twenty-five times more than the man ever possessed or ever will possess. Well, the common sense of the other Mangyan(s) told them that Sabong was wrong. He was asked to return the amount he had collected which he refused to do...[10]

The seeming benevolence of the Americans, their eagerness to protect the Mangyans from "lowland Tagalog" exploitation widened the already existing gap between lowland and inland groups in Mindoro. In fact, the early American tribal policies encouraged the isolation of pagan and Muslim groups from the greater mass of Philippine society. Merton Miller, acting chief of the Ethnological Survey at that time proposed that Mangyans be organized into settlements and be kept as far away as possible from the influence of Tagalogs.[11] The Americans thus initially favored isolation rather than admixture of pagan and Christian groups for obvious reasons— a people divided cannot effectively press for freedom. A report of the Philippine Commission in 1921 cited for instance that:

> ...the pagans and non-Christians, constituting about 10 percent of the population, are for continued American control. They want peace and security. These the Americans have given them.[12]

[9] Fletcher Gardner, M-P Paper No. 2, p. 33.
[10] *Ibid.*, p. 15.
[11] Merton Miller in "Letters Relating to the Mangyans of Mindoro," M-P, *op. cit.*, p. 35.
[12] The Bacon Bill of 1926, for instance, proposed to separate Mindanao and

In seeking to win the confidence of pagan and Muslim groups, the Americans further exacerbated the rift between these people and the majority lowland group. In the case of the Mangyans, the formation of settlements "away from the Tagalogs" heightened their separation from the Christian majority, a separation initially brought about by Spain.

It must be pointed out that, in the formation of such settlements, the Americans did not hesitate to use sheriff force to compel the Mangyans to remain in the area and also to bring back those who escaped from it. For instance, the decision in a lawsuit filed against the provincial board of Mindoro concerning the use of sheriff force, reiterated that it was legal to do so. Section 4 of the Supreme Court decision in fact defined that the Mangyans may be imprisoned for failure to comply with the policy, stating that:

> The action to compel a non-Christian to take up their habitation to a certain place, under penalty of imprisonment for failure of member to do so was authorized by the provincial board (i.e., Mindoro Provincial Board), duly approved by the Secretary of Interior...[13]

Accordingly, one Mangyan who had escaped from the reservation was arrested and jailed by the sheriff.

American policy toward the Mangyans was rooted in the view that the Mangyans, "being of a low grade of civilization," did not deserve the same rights as the "Filipinos." The same Supreme Court decision opines that:

> Theoretically, all men are created free and equal. Practically we know that the axiom is not precisely accurate. The Mangyans, for instance, are not free, as civilized men are free, and they are not the equals of their more fortunate brothers. True indeed, they are citizens, with many but not all the rights which citizenship implies... But just as surely, the Manguianes are citizens of a low degree of intelligence, and Filipinos who are a drag upon the progress of the State...[14]

With the coming of the Americans, therefore, the Mangyans became more distinct as a people not equal to the Mindoro lowlanders.

Sulu from the remainder of the Archipelago and permanently retain these rich islands under American sovereignty. *Report of the Special Mission to the Philippine Islands to the Secretary of War* (Washington: Government Printing Office, 1922), p. 45.

[13] Edmond Block and H. Lawrence Noble, *Digest of the Reports of the Supreme Court of the Philippine Islands*, Vol. 4 (Rochester, New York; The Lawyers Co-Operative Publishing Company, 1927), p. 3230.

[14] *Ibid.*, p. 3231.

The view of the Mangyans as an inferior people, the promulgation of specialized laws and government for them, the creation of settlements away from the "Tagalog Filipinos" — all led to the growing awareness that they were a minority in the land.

PRESSURES FROM CHRISTIAN LOWLANDERS

Despite the efforts of the Americans to wean away the Mangyans from the hold of the lowlanders, the latter's parasitic relations with them persisted and became more intensified under the new regime. A letter of Merton Miller in 1904 cited, for instance, how a whole town lived principally by trading cloth, bolos, beads and earthen vessels with the Mangyans who grew the crops essentially meant for them. Such practice led him to conclude that the Mangyans

> ...did most of the work in the region and that the Christian Filipino lived on the industry of the Mangyans.[15]

Exposed more extensively to the southern Mangyans, Gardner noted how these people were much oppressed by fictitious debts with which they were charged by their Tagalog and Bisayan neighbors. He noted that:

> They are compelled to cultivate the fields of the coast natives, and to bring in tribute of bees wax, honey crops from their own fields. Strong efforts have been made by the Provincial authorities to break up this practice so demoralizing to both parties, but evidence is hard to procure.[16]

Another convenient way by which lowlanders exploited the "Hampangan" Mangyan was the rite of *sanduguan* or blood-brotherhood, where blood taken from the arm or breast was drunk by each participant, thereby forging a "compact which endures until death." Describing an aspect of the compact, Gardner reports that

> ...If it becomes necessary that an enemy should be killed it is possible to get a blood brother among the Mangyans to accomplish it. If at any time, a blood brother's life is in danger a blood brother earns (?) him and will never leave him until the threatened danger is passed.[17]

The rite, however, held no meaning for the lowlander except that of his own gain, "and the simpler mountain dweller is thoroughly cheated in the long run." What was thus conceived as noble by the

---

[15] Merton Miller, M-P Paper No. 2, p. 24.
[16] Fletcher Gardner, *op. cit.*, p. 6.
[17] *Ibid.*, p. 24.

Mangyans was turned into a convenient tool for exploitation by their lowland kins. Among the Mangyan blood-brothers, however, the exalted rite was fulfilled with almost fanatical devotion that even the "poorest always have rice on hand for the *sandugo* when he comes to visit, even at the time of the greatest scarcity of food."[18]

Apart from the rite of *sanduguan,* the Mangyans likewise fell prey to various rackets made by wily lowlanders. Reports given by the Americans noted how on different occasions, lowlanders obtained goods and money by taking advantage of Mangyan ignorance and superstition. One such incident described in a court case involved a Mangyan who was induced to accept at the price of a carabao a certain piece of paper which allegedly would be changed into some

> coin paper and silver money after the lapse of seven (Friday(s), provided that on each of said Friday he would offer appropriate prayers for the success of the enterprise, and that said paper would make him a rich man, without any other consideration than said paper . . .[19]

In most cases, lowland-Mangyan interaction always bred destructive effects among these mountain people. Some, due to exposure to lowland practices, learned how to drink and gamble. Ordoñez, one time presidente of Bulalacao reported how the Hanunoo and Bukid peoples learned to play *monte* from a lowland adventurer who leeched them of their small possessions. In his account,

> ... prior to few years ago the people we are discussing knew no game of cards, but they learned how to play monte from an adventurer ... that adventurer merely by playing monte with the Bukid won some dozen cavans of cacao, from which he made a neat little sum of money. The Hanono-o and Bukid now know cards and how to play them. They also take part in the game of checks . . .[20]

Though some Mangyans maintained relatively close contact with the lowlanders, the majority chose to remain out of the sphere of lowland influence. Among the Mangyans in Mansalay, this was expressly stated in some writings on bamboo tubes done by Luyon and collected and translated by Gardner in 1906. One of these says:

---

[18] Niurio Ordoñez, "Report on the Mangyan Tribes of Mindoro," *op. cit.,* M-P Paper No. 3, p. 3.
[19] *Philippine Reports, op. cit.,* p. 3231. This case of course shows how this particular Mangyan is already on the verge of becoming integrated into lowland belief system.
[20] Niurio Ordoñez, "Report on the Mangyan Tribes of Mindoro," *op. cit.,* M-P Paper No. 3, p. 1.

> We Hanono-o Mangyans here at Mansalay do not allow our children to go to the town to work for the Christians even though they might learn a gainful trade, and get clothing and whatever else can be named.[21]

The passage clearly reflects Mangyan distrust of townspeople born undoubtedly out of age-old dealings with the *damuongs*[22] or lowlanders. The sub-human treatment of the Mangyans by lowlanders may be further gleaned from the passage which follows:

> Ti damoong unman magasawa sa kanmi no totoo umasawa agugman di man may daraga Mangyan nagasawa sa damoong sitay sa Mansalay dapat ti damoong nagkaanak sa kami sa kay pagtukadtukad sa bantud.[23]

In brief, the text states that the lowlanders never take the Mangyans in true matrimony—the Christians beget children among them as "they climb through hills." In other words, the Mangyans were never considered worthy of matrimony. They were, in the eyes of the lowlanders, only fit for "sexual escapade." Thus, the class distinctions laid out in the Spanish era became more pronounced during the American colonial regime. The Mangyans, in response to the subhuman treatment accorded them became more wary about entering into a tenant-landlord relationship with them. In the words of Luyon, the Hanunoo Mangyans had learned to perceive lowland deception and they no longer wished to follow any master and be aggrieved in the partition of farm produce.

Yet, self-sufficient as they were, the Hanunoo themselves saw the necessity of maintaining trade relations with the lowlanders. From the same Luyon, we learn that

> ... all the Mangyans (referring to Mangyans in Mansalay) plant rice ... We keep for ourselves of the harvest just one-half for eating and sell only one-half to the Christians... This part is carried always to the

---

[21] Fletcher Gardner, *Indic Writings*, p. 67.

[22] This word, according to Postma, comes from the root *duong*, "to land from a boat." Thus *damuong* literally means "those who have come by boat," evidently in contrast to the Hanunoo who had "always been there." Today, *damuong* is the designation for all non-Mangyans whom they took upon as outsiders and intruders. (Antoon Postma S. "Development among the Mangyans," *Philippine Quarterly of Culture and Society*, Vol. 2, Nos. 1-2, offprint copy, p. 24). Conklin, on the other hand, defines the word as "Stranger," or "any Tagalog or other Christian lowlander who may be distinguished from the mountain pagans by short hair (males), Christian dress and strange (to Hanunoo) customs and habits" *Hanunoo-English Vocabulary* (Berkeley: UCLA Press, 1953). In Tagalog, "to land with a boat" is *"daung."*

[23] Gardner, *Indic Writings*, p. 67.

town, like cacao, maize and tobacco where we always exchange it for cloth, bolos, bead necklace, and for anything else...[24]

As in other areas of lowland-Mangyan relations, the exchange of goods itself served as a handy means for further profit-making on the part of the lowlanders. In the words of Gardner, the Mangyans

> nearly always take their pay in cloth beads, little belts, rings, and salt, which affords ample opportunity to the tiendas to clear a still larger profit.[25]

Profit-making also took other forms like underpaying the Mangyans for their labor, or not paying them at all. Most cases tried by Offley in his capacity as Mangyan governor usually revolved around this issue. In a report dated July 10, 1904, he described one such case

> ...wherein a Mangyan was promised a "chupa" of sea salt for a banco (i.e., *banca*—V.B.L.) fifty feet long complaining only because the salt had not been paid. As he proved that he had performed other labor for the same man, a Filipino, he was given judgment for ₱120.00, which was paid and in my hands, to be spent by him in my presence to assure fair treatment otherwise he would pay the whole amount for a 40 cent bolo...[26]

The usurious practice of the lowlanders served equally as a strong snare for the naive Mangyan mind. Under this system, as Offley further described it,

> ...The tao borrows a peso or two and gives one of his numerous children as a guarantee of payment. This child becomes the household slave and is allowed a credit of 50 centavos a month for its labor. But the child must eat and have a new shirt occasionally, the cost of which is added to the original debt, and by some means of reckoning the original 2 pesos becomes 72 at the end of a year. The debt continues to grow, though its payment in cash is not desired and is passed down from one generation to another.[27]

In relation to the case cited above, Offley reported one instance where two "Filipinos" were prosecuted by him, "for kidnapping Manguian children for an alleged debt of the father," while in another

---

[24] *Ibid.*, p. 51.
[25] Gardner, M-P Paper No. 2, p. 4.
[26] "Report of the Governor of the Province of Mindoro" in *Annual Reports of the War Department,* Vol. 10, Part 1 (Washington: Government Printing Office, 1905), p. 316.
[27] "Report of the Philippine Commission" in *Annual Reports of the War Department,"* Vol. 11, Part 1 (Washington: Government Printing Office, 1905), p. 542.

case, the accused acknowledged that the father worked for him eight years in payment "for a sinamay shirt" the local value of which was 75 centavo Mexican, but still it was claimed the shirt had not been paid for.28

One of the more compelling forces encountered by the Mangyans in this period was the influx of Tagalog, Visayan, and Ilocano migrants. With the improved means of transportation to and from the surrounding regions and the general well-being of the coastal residents, the number of migrants from other provinces increased. Worcester, writing on the over-all achievements of the colonial government in Mindoro, noted that between 1913 and 1929,

> ... An excellent state of public order has been established, and there has not been an armed ladrone (i.e., bandit) in the province for years. It was famous for its "bad climate." We have shown that its climate is good, making its own (sic) really healthful by merely cleaning them up.29

While this improvement proved beneficial for the coastal dwellers, it gave rise to manifold problems for the Mangyans who were faced with an ever-increasing number of land-hungry settlers who took every opportunity to grab the lands cleared and cultivated by them. The annual report of the Secretary of the Interior for the fiscal year of 1913 cited that

> ... When members of non-Christian tribes are persuaded to give up nomadic habits and permanently settle on lands which it is desired that they should be allowed to cultivate, the question of conveying their titles to such lands is one which presents serious difficulties. The semi-nomadic habits of many of these tribes are largely due to the fact that as soon as they have cleared the land and brought it under cultivation they are driven from it by false claims of ownership on the part of their civilized neighbors.30

In 1925, land conflicts were noted as increasing in the annual report of the Philippine Commission due to the "intrusion of Christian home seekers over homesteads already occupied by non-Christians."31 To protect the interests of the Mangyans and other ethnic groups

---

28 *Ibid.*
29 Dean C. Worcester, *The Philippines: Past and Present* (New York: the Macmillan Company, 1934), p. 464.
30 "Report of the Secretary of the Interior," in *Report of the Philippine Commission, 1913* (Washington: Government Printing Office, 1914), p. 92.
31 "Report of the Secretary of the Interior," in *Report of the Philippine Commission, 1925* (Washington: Government Printing Office, 1926), p. 262.

classified under the regular provinces, a new policy was inaugurated by the Bureau of non-Christian tribes. It was agreed with the officials of the regularly organized provinces that

> (1) the bureau of non-Christian tribes through the provincial governor, shall exercise control and supervision over the territory inhabited by non-Christians in these provinces.
>
> (2) the provincial board and the provincial governor will transact business with the bureau in all matters affecting territories inhabited by non-Christians of said Provinces in the same manner as they deal with the executive bureau with respect to matters affecting the regularly organized Provinces.[32]

Though it cannot be denied that the Americans tried to solve the problem of land-grabbing, no lasting solution was effected for they failed to provide the Mangyans with sufficient incentives for permanent settlement. Faulty communication of changes intended for these people, aggravated by the attendant use of police force in the establishment of settlements, alienated rather than won them over to measures designed to protect them from land-hungry migrants.

The coming of the Japanese in 1942 further intensified lowland encroachments on Mangyan territory, as coastal residents evacuated into the interior to avoid the terrorism by the new colonial power. Save for some who were captured, taken as captives and made to fight in the war, most of the Mangyans found refuge in the deep jungles of Mt. Halcon.

As the Japanese rule was short-lived, and their interest was primarily to stabilize their rule and extract maximum economic benefits from the archipelago in line with the Greater East Asia Co-Prosperity Sphere, no direct assault was made on the Mangyans hidden in the interior.

The post-War reports on the lowland-Mangyan relations give a clear picture of the perpetuation and, in fact, the intensification of the manifold pressures which had accumulated during the American colonial regime. Following their goal of reaching out to these people, a team of Protestant missionaries did a thorough survey of the Mangyan region in 1951. Marked exploitation of these people was observed in terms of labor, land and purchase of goods. In brief, the team reported that

[32] *Ibid.*

> ..."Christiano" farmers persuade them to do rough work in their farms and then give them little more than their food for their wages. The government has set aside reservations for them, but frequently, the government agent persuades the Mangyans, who have cleared a piece of this land for farming purposes, to sell it for a small sum. Fearing to disobey the government-appointed agent, superintendent of the Mangyan, the tribesman will sell this land for a few pesos. The agent will then sell it to a neighboring "Christiano" farmer for a much higher figure.[33]

At this point then, lowland pressure doubled to include even the government-appointed agents. Interviews made by the survey team further described these as

> ...not too interested in the enlightenment of the Mangyans. So long as they are ignorant they are easy to exploit... They will block your efforts (referring to planned missionary out-reach among the Mangyans) and give you endless trouble, unless they know that what you are doing is with the hearty concurrence and express permission of the top authorities in the nation's capital...[34]

Thus, the very people assigned to protect the Mangyans were themselves a primary source of exploitation. A CNI representative to the Mangyans, after gaining their confidence, cheated them of the money he collected for the supposed processing of their application for land titles. Of this sad experience with government agents, one missionary to the Tadyawan wrote that it was not easy for "the Tadyawan to trust the outside world," because

> ...the outside world had done nothing to inspire trust, but, on the contrary, had taken every possible advantage of the timid tribesman, cheating him, tricking him, and making unreasonable demands upon him and his time. Initially we had been happy to cooperate with the government's program of integration, but how could we go on wholeheartedly encouraging it when it meant nothing but heartache upon heartache for the tribesman...[35]

As of old, the ordinary lowlanders were likewise a constant source of pressures. Carolyn Stickley, a missionary who lived among the Tadyawans and other tribes for an extended period of time, took note of

---

[33] "Philippine Island Survey Report for the China Inland Mission," April 30-July 6, 1951, original manuscript, p. 9.
[34] *Ibid.*
[35] Caroline Stickley, *Broken Snare* (London: O.M.F. Books, January 1975), p. 193.

> ...a steadily growing stream of Filipinos (who) invaded the mountains in quest of land, imposing on the tribesmen and taking advantage of them. It was a grievous burden, and the tribesmen's minds were troubled....[36]

The land problem was not confined only to the Tadyawan but was happening all over the island of Mindoro, for

> ...Filipinos invaded the mountains, carrying false pieces of papers, shoving them under the noses of illiterate tribesmen and telling them it was their deed to the land the tribesmen were living on and that they have to leave. Others came in and offered the tribesman a small sum of money for his long-cultivated land, and the tribesman, ignorant of the value of money and thinking he was rich, would accept the pittance and move off the land, unknowingly forfeiting his privilege of squatter's right to the only land he could legally claim...[37]

Mangyan responses to these pressures ranged from withdrawal through seclusion, to assimilation. There was only one case recorded of violent retaliation and this took place during the early years of American rule. Gardner recounts that

> ...Just a few years ago, a Spaniard, living in Bulalacao, had enslaved a Mangyan girl. The Spaniard was notified by the girl's family and friends, to return her to her home. The Spaniard took no notice whatever of the warning (sic)...A second, and a third time he was requested to return the girl. The Spaniard only took the precaution to go armed. One day as he was passing across a high narrow point, he was slain by the Mangyans, who had concealed themselves among the rocks.
>
> This occurred in 1901. This act of primitive justice aroused considerable fear among the Filipinos, who yet speak of these Mangyans as dangerous characters. These particular Mangyans, after killing the Spaniard, retired to the mountains to the north of Bating (Bagting?) and since then, have had little to do with the outside population. While this event is not an exhibition of blood-thirstiness, it does exhibit unexpected traits in them. The action of the Spaniard also served to make them suspicious of outsiders.[38]

"Withdrawal" as a form of response seemed to be "the only one solution" for the Tadyawan as well as for others, since, living

> ...so close to the large river, they were too accessible to the outside world; they knew they would have to move deeper into the mountains.[39]

[36] *Ibid.*, p. 114.
[37] *Ibid.*, p. 176.
[38] Fletcher Gardner, "The Mangyans," M-P Paper No. 2, *op. cit.*, p. 4.
[39] *Ibid.*, p. 114.

Among the Hanunoo, the characteristic response has been that of relative seclusion. While a few maintained social contact with the lowlanders for trade in order to exchange their agricultural products for "non-agricultural necessities," the rest of the Hanunoo population chose to avoid unnecessary contact with lowlanders. This, of course, led to the relative isolation of the group, despite their proximity to Christian villages. As Conklin recorded in 1954,

> Knowledge of the outside world is limited largely to what is heard and observed in the few Christian settlements, and what visitors (traders, occasional hunters, missionaries, and anthropologists) tell them. Most of what they do know about Christian Filipino culture, they dislike, distrust, and often fear. Because of their even stronger passion for peace, however, these sentiments are not openly proclaimed or fought for. Instead every precaution is taken to avoid such conflict by avoiding unnecessary contact with lowlanders...[40]

This isolationist attitude of the Hanunoo led, according to Conklin, to "pronounced culture lag." In particular,

> Political trends and social changes among the Christian Filipinos have virtually no direct effect on Hanunoo daily life. Although some syncretism of Hanunoo and lowland culture has taken place, it has done so very gradually and with pronounced culture lag. There are numerous indications that the Hanunoo retain much of what may be considered pre-Spanish Visayan, or central Philippine culture.[41]

Convenient as it might have been in the past, the age-old mountain retreats of the Mangyans can no longer give them the isolation they formerly enjoyed. As Antoon Postma explained in an article,

> ...With the rapid growth of its population now taking place, at least among the lowland Filipinos, these have encroached more and more upon the remaining Mangyan territory. The latter can thus no longer maintain their "splendid isolation" and continue in their own cherished ways. The twentieth century has at long last caught up with them and, in one way or another, they will have to come to terms with it. Since they are by geographic accident part of the Republic of the Philippines, they can no longer persist in their traditional refusal to be governed by its law and regulations.[42]

The Mangyans have entered a new era—an age that will not leave them in peace. On the one hand, there is the government pressure

---

[40] Conklin, Hanunoo Culture, p. 58.
[41] *Ibid.*, p. 59.
[42] Antoon Postma, "Development Among the Mangyans," *op. cit.*, p. 23.

for them to integrate. On the other hand, there is the unabated encroachment on their territory by lowland Filipinos. It is, as Postma succinctly puts it, "the old, sad story of the encounter between an advanced civilization and a primitive culture, which recurs throughout the history of mankind."[43] The Mangyans, like all minority groups with a less technologically developed culture, "have lost much more than they gained from the encounter."[44]

REPERCUSSIONS FROM EVANGELIZATION

The introduction of the American policy of separation between Church and State saw a momentary weakening of the religious impact in Mindoro. Stripped of their former rights, save the propagation of the Catholic faith, the once powerful friars were relegated to mere spiritual administrators. The reorganization of the Philippine Church in June 1902 by Pope Leo XIII further reduced religious activity in the island, as Mindoro fell under the jurisdiction of the diocese of Lipa. This, coupled with the restriction on the Recollects' ministry in Palawan, aggravated the perennial scarcity of religious workers in Mindoro. Missionary activity in the island was so reduced that concentrated and full-time religious work was restored only in 1936 with the creation of Mindoro as an apostolic-prefecture under the Society of the Divine Word, a German Catholic mission.

A review of the spiritual accomplishments of the Catholic Church in Mindoro during the American colonial regime reflects a general weakening of the religious pressure on the Mangyans. In contrast to this, work among the already Christian lowlanders was greatly increased, leading to the establishment of a number of Catholic schools and the organization of the laity into numerous church groups. Among the Church's activities listed by Landicho at this time,[45] not one seems to have directly affected the Mangyans. This seeming lack of missionary zeal for work among the pagans of Mindoro may have been partly due to the fact that the American colonizers were themselves greatly preoccupied with their welfare. In a word, the American policy of isolation rather than admixture of lowlanders and Mangyans, coupled with the separation of the Church and the State, cut off the Mangyans

---

[43] *Ibid.*
[44] *Ibid.*
[45] Macario Z. Landicho, "Ecclesiastical Administration" in *Mindoro Yearbook* (Manila: Year Book Publishers, 1952), pp. 136-38.

from intensive religious influence. On the other hand, the age-old experience of sub-human treatment by Christian lowlanders, dating as far back as the Spanish colonial regime, had turned the Mangyan's mind away from the Gospel and even from becoming a convert of the coastal resident's form of Christianity. In fact, the lament of present-day missionaries faced with Mangyans who have turned stone-cold to the Gospel is but an echo of the dirge sung by the Spanish friars.

In his time, Gardner found traces of Catholic penetration among the Mangyans. He believed that

> ... they have been at some time under the influence of the Friars, as they related to me the legends of Adam and Eve, and of the Tower of Babel....
>
> They believe certain beings, one of whom is their "Ama" or Father, will not allow them to remain long in the towns, and if they disobey gives them wryneck. Like other natives, they fear something lives in the Balete trees, and of whom they ask permission in passing. They described it as small and malevolent. They believe in the Aswang, the mamao, and in the tic-balan, kapre, or oco (?) ...[46]

Faced constantly with the reality of lowland encroachment on their rights and property, the Hampangan or Hanunoo's system of beliefs made room for teachings against prolonged contact with the townspeople. When some beliefs do not present an immediate threat to the group's security, Mangyan religion absorbed them, particularly those which could explain in part their experiences in the forest, thus leading to syncretic religious forms.

Concentrated efforts in reaching the Mangyans with the Christian gospel was revived only in the '50s. The reason for this long delay was summed up in a report of a survey by the China Inland Mission. The report concludes that

> It cannot be said that *no* attempts have been made to reach the highland peoples of the Philippines with the Gospel. It can be said that only very little is being done now. The missionary staff in the Philippines is small. Most missionaries seem overworked. The larger number appear to be engaged in school work or institutional work of various kinds... The Filipino Church seems engrossed with its own post-war problems and has little strength to reach out even to fellow Filipinos, much less to concern itself with "those people" up in the hills. The chief barrier in the way of reaching (out) ... is their inaccessibility and the linguis-

[46] Fletcher Gardner "Letters Relating to the Mangyans," M-P Paper No. 3, p. 1.

tic problems involved. Few in the Philippine Islands today have the necessary time and strength and money to interest themselves in the spiritual warfare of the pagan tribes. The Roman Catholics have made a few efforts to convert some of them, especially in Mt. Province of Luzon, but the ones they are reaching now are the ones on the fringes of civilization—those who went to towns and cities for the purposes of trade...[47]

Among the first to resume active missionary work among the Mangyans, particularly among the Hanunoo, were the workers of the New Tribes Mission. The work of this Protestant group started early in the '50s but this was later ceded to the Overseas Missionary Fellowship to allow for more integrated tribal work in the region.

The work of the O.M.F. among the Mangyans officially began in April 1952, as Frances Williamson and Marie Barham started work among the Iraya people located in Saclag. This place was a two-hour trek from San Teodoro, the first O.M.F. base.

Four years after its inception, the O.M.F. missionary efforts were reported to have branched out to the other Mangyan groups including the Bangon, Alagan, "Batangan," Nauhan-Pola, Hanunoo, Buhid and Ratagnon. At least two missionaries in each tribe were reported to be actively at work not only in evangelization but also the translation of portions of the Scriptures in the different Mangyan dialects. Translations done with the aid of the Mangyans themselves have, in the words of Hazel Page,

> ...made it possible to give stronger emphasis to our teaching for we can rely on the power of His word. As a result of the Word working in lives, growth has been evident in the believers...[48]

Yet some of the other Mangyan groups have not needed as much translation as the Hanunoo. As one report emphasized

> ...Many Iraya churches... use Tagalog in their services and read and understand the Tagalog Bible. The Alangan are gradually using more Tagalog. But not the Hanunoo. They are proud of being Hanunoo. They want to hold onto their language and also their tribal dress. So every effort was made to give them the hymns and Scriptures they needed for their services in Hanunoo.[49]

---

[47] "Philippine Islands Survey Report," *op. cit.*
[48] Cited in May Johnston's forthcoming book tentatively entitled "Mindoro's Gold," original manuscript, p. 14.
[49] *Ibid.*, p. 7.

The general policy, however, has been to reach the varying Mangyan groups in their own tongues, despite the marked spread of Tagalog as lingua franca among the Mangyans.

As the missionaries sought to reinforce basic pride in Mangyan culture, efforts were also made to discourage practices contrary to the Christian teachings. The product of the missionary work among the Mangyans may be inferred from the missionary work among the Buhids. When the missionaries first reached them,

> ... most settlements had only two or three huts. The huts were scattered because with death, everyone left the area. Sometimes if they see that death is approaching they carry the sick one to a little shelter in the forest. If the person dies in a hut, it is abandoned and the vicinity is avoided for fear of the spirits. The one who handles the dead body of a person is under a taboo for nine days. He must not touch any other person until the nine days are ended by a feast and ceremonial washing. This often meant that a poor weak widow had to struggle alone to carry the dead body of her husband to the burial place.
>
> For the Christians, this has all changed. The believers can show that they do not now fear death. They often help to dig the grave and carry the dead. The unbelievers are impressed by these social improvements in the tribe... Larger settlements are now growing up, and when the heathen see that the believers do not run away after a death or after calamity happens to them, they are emboldened to remain also...[50]

In the area of marriage, the missionaries have also tried to impart the Christian concept of fidelity and monogamy. For in practice, the Buhid

> ... have never looked upon marriage as binding and the concept of being faithful to one partner for life is something new to their culture. If parents do not like a son-in-law they will bring pressure upon the daughter to leave him and find another husband. This has become a real problem among the Christians.[51]

The actual effect on and responses of the Mangyans to all these introduced changes can, of course, be seen only from the particular perspective of missionary ethics and beliefs. On the socio-anthropological level, it may still be too early to assess the impact of missionary ingress into Mangyan life. The positive and negative effects could only be gauged, in the final analysis, by the Mangyans themselves as the act vis-a-vis the new Christian penetration. For the

---

[50] *Ibid.*, p. 56.
[51] *Ibid.*

moment, they appear to view the mission as a counterpoise to the traditional threats to their life ways and individual interests.

One of the major achievements of the O.M.F. missionaries in their work among the different Mangyan tribes was the establishment of an inter-tribal fellowship of believers. This was effected through the annual Mangyan Church conferences that sought to bring together representatives from the different Mangyan groups. During such conferences, led and later organized by the Mangyans themselves, the social and spiritual problems of the different local churches are discussed together with the strategy for future evangelization work among the isolated groups. In their sixth annual conference, this inter-tribal group was duly incorporated and assumed legal status. Thus, with the guidance and help of the missionaries, the *Samahan ng mga Pantribong Iglesiyang Ebanhelika ng Mangyan*, the first inter-tribal Mangyan association of its kind, came into being.

To further provide biblical training for the emerging Mangyan leaders, the O.M.F. workers encouraged the establishment of a Mangyan Bible School under the sponsorship of the newly-established Mangyan association. The Bible School was planned for recognized leaders, especially among the young men who might become church elders, deacons, or evangelists. Married men were also considered, along with their families, if housing was available. To make this venture self-sufficient and not dependent on outside help, each Mangyan group is encouraged to sponsor its own chosen "student." In addition, land purchased out of an initial donation and jointly cultivated by the students after their academic work for the day serves as a major source of food supply.

A major policy of the school which indirectly encourages integration into lowland culture is the use of Tagalog as a medium for communication. May Johnston, evangelical missionary, reports among the Mangyans that since

> ... the tribal languages were not mutually understood, Tagalog, the language spoken by most lowland Filipinos in Mindoro, was chosen as the medium of instruction. The requirements weren't too exacting but perhaps to many Mangyans, they appeared to be. A student needed to have a working knowledge of Tagalog, a fair ability to read and preferably to write also, and some foundation knowledge of scripture truth.[52]

[52] *Ibid.*, p. 2.

Since its inception, the Mangyan Bible School has provided training for a significant number of graduates who have since gone back to their own ethnic groups and begun ministry among their own people.

A record of missionary activity among the Mangyans is not complete without reference to the work of Fr. Antoon Postma, begun in 1958. Unlike the Protestant missionaries, Fr. Postma chose to concentrate his work among the Hanunoo in Mansalay, Oriental Mindoro. A start was made, not with a ready proclamation of the Gospel, but with a determined effort to understand "the mentality of the Mangyans and the expressions of their culture." This was achieved through a painstaking study of the Hanunoo language and script, as well as the *ambahan*, "a song-poem that seemed to accompany their life on all important occasions." While trying to get the expressions of their mind, Postma also tried to induce the Hanunoo parents to send their children to the elementary public school in Mansalay. When these initial attempts towards Hanunoo education failed, efforts were shifted to the establishment of a school back in the mountain area. In taking these steps, Postma was guided by the principle that education is the first step towards development and integration. With great difficulty and accompanying conflicts with existing traditions, this view was effectively carried out. As Postma himself wrote,

> Notwithstanding all these setbacks and difficulties, modern education has already proven its value in promoting development among the Mangyans, and the influence of the school is greater that (sic) one might think. Everytime the children go home, they take with them their newly-acquired concepts about modern civilizations, government institutions, cleanliness and proper hygiene, things unknown to the old generation, but already a part of daily life for the young people.[53]

The method, of course, follows the long-standing Catholic practice consecrated by history itself. Among others, the Jesuits pioneered in it from the very start of the 17th century in the Philippines.[54] In general, the Catholic missionaries of the early heroic age integrated themselves

---

[53] Antoon Postma, "Development Among the Mangyans," *Philippine Quarterly of Culture and Society*, Vol. 2, Nos. 1-2, offprint copy.
[54] Cf. Horacio de la Costa, *The Jesuits in the Philippines. 1581-1768* (Cambridge, Mass.: Harvard University Press, 1961). In general, the Catholic missionaries of the early heroic age integrated themselves first into their "mission" communities before initiating a strategy of attraction among the chiefs and leaders, and among the children.

first into their mission communities before initiating a strategy of attraction among the chiefs and leaders as well as the children.

Though limited in extent, the experience of the Hanunoo under Postma's guidance illustrated the effectiveness of his missionary approach. This, of course, led to diverse changes in Hanunoo life, including the establishment of residential community organizations. Contrary to the traditional Mangyan way of building their dwellings near the fields, Postma pioneered in building a village around a school-clinic-chapel complex, analogous to the *reducción* in Spanish times. This set-up, according to Postma, "gives the Mangyans not only the benefits to be derived from these institutions, but also the chance to learn from each other the many different new ways that are presented to them." With these new ways, a modern form of leadership is introduced—a system based on elections rather than on the traditional choice emphasizing age and experience. This change in the socio-political structure of the Mangyans of Mansalay was a welcome one; not only was the village created as an official barrio, the villagers were also allowed to elect the barrio officials from among themselves. Postma described this first regular election of barrio officials as "quite a boost to the Mangyan community," making

> ...them realize that they were accepted as the equals of other communities within the town and Philippine society at large. Moreover, the use of Mangyan script during the election, probably the first *official* use ever made of it was another instance fostering the integration of Mangyan culture into modern Philippine culture.[55]

Clearly, Postma's strategy for evangelization centered around alleviating the Mangyans' social ills first before presenting the person of Jesus Christ. "It was as a Christian and a missionary," he says, "that I undertook the task of helping the Mangyans on the painful road towards integration with the rest of the nation." He believes that a satisfactory integration into the national community "must be accompanied by a solid moral formation rooted in religious convictions, if it is to last." Thus, alongside social action, Postma undertook to share the good news of God's personal interest and love expressed historically in Christ, being himself personally

---

[55] Postma, *loc. cit.*, p. 29.

...convinced that Christianity will give the Mangyans the moral support they need in choosing what is valuable in modern civilization, without losing their identity and self-esteem, and in this way ensure their development as full-fledged members of the wider community of which they are a part.[56]

The age-old zeal of missionaries for Mangyan conversion, the new yet historically based pressures from the American colonial enterprise on the one hand, and the Christianized-Westernized lowlanders on the other, constituted the old and new forces that encroached on Mangyan life. The Mangyan responses to these pressures have been as varied as the pressures themselves. Imitation, withdrawal, resistance, isolation, and submission are but some of the manifold Mangyan responses to pressures from within and without the world they live and move in.

[56] *Ibid.*, p. 31.

Chapter Five

Towards the Idea
of Integration

INTENSIFIED by admixture with Chinese and European blood, the diversity of the people of the Philippines was readily recognized as a potential source of social conflicts by the Americans. In particular, the new colonial masters focused their attention on the existence of a "substantial" minority consisting of the "pagan" and Muslim groups. The keen awareness that these people were different and posed a problem similar to that of the Indians in the United States led them to work out policies that initially defined majority-minority relations.

As an innovation to the Spanish classification of the inhabitants in ecclesiastical terms—that is, dividing the people into Christians, *infieles* (heathen), and *moros,* the Americans formulated the term "non-Christian" to

> designate the pagan and Muslim groups in distinction from the Christian Filipinos dwelling in organized provinces and towns, for whom a frame of government had been practically completed as early as a year ago. (i.e., 1901—V.B.L.)[1]

With this act, the Americans formally set the distinction between lowlanders and highlanders, "Christians" and Muslims. In fact, the term "Filipino" was solely used to signify the majority, lowland

[1] Report of the Chief of the Bureau of Non-Christian Tribes for the Year Ending August 31, 1902 included in the *Third Annual Report of the Philippine Commission 1902* Part 1, Bureau of Insular Affairs, War Department (Washington: Government Printing Office, 1903), p. 679.

Christian groups. The term "non-Christian," however, was stripped of its religious undertones or its literal meaning. In a Supreme Court case, "Ruby vs. the Provincial Board of Mindoro" involving the Mangyans, it was expressly pointed out that the term was intended to relate to the degree of civilization and not to religious beliefs. As defined in the court decision, the term should refer particularly to geographical area, "and more directly to the natives of the Philippine Islands of a low grade of civilization."[2]

The colonial government took a further step by creating the Bureau of Non-Christian Tribes on October 2, 1901. Its objectives, as stated in the organizing act, were: (1) to investigate the actual condition of the pagan and Mohammedan tribes and consequently make recommendations for legislation by the civil government and (2) to conduct scientific investigations in the ethnology of the country.[3]

Yet, as pointed out later by Merton Miller, the goal was not merely scientific but likewise political, since

> ...An acquaintance with the non-Christian tribes, with their customs and ideas, would make it possible to govern them better and more easily than would otherwise be possible....[4]

This new emphasis on the use of scientific findings for administration of minorities was a lesson learned from the blunders made in administering the Indians. This was expressly stated in the initial report of Dr. David Barrows, chief of the Bureau who wrote that

> The variety of problems they present is equally for the ethnologist and statesman, and nowhere, it may be asserted, must the constructive work of administration be so dependent for information and guidance upon the researches of the expert... Out of mutual ignorance and fear have followed hatred, oppression and retaliation. In the establishment of order in these islands this government is attempting to rear a new standard for relationship between the white man and the Malay. The success of this effort will depend in a large measure on our understanding and scientific grasp of the peoples whose problems we are facing.[5]

---

[2] Edmond Block and H. L. Noble, *Digest of the Reports of the Supreme Court of the Philippine Islands*, Vol. 4 (Rochester, New York: The Lawyers Co-Operative Publishing Company, 1927), p. 3230.
[3] *Third Annual Report of the Philippine Commission, op. cit.*
[4] *Fourth Annual Report of the Philippine Commission*, 1904, Part 2 (Washington: Government Printing Office, 1905), p. 571.
[5] *Third Annual Report of the Philippine Commission, op. cit.*, p. 679.

Under instructions from the Philippine Commission, Barrows visited and made investigations in Indian reservations and schools in the United States. The trip was designed primarily to gain information concerning the results obtained by the administration of Indian affairs. On the basis of this study, Barrows proposed that since the new U.S. policy of breaking down tribal ties and dealing with the Indians as individuals rather than as tribes had failed, it could not work out as well in the Philippines. As he expressed it in his report,

> ...In spite of the excellent intentions behind these efforts, the policy... has not brought forth satisfactory results, and in a thousand cases has not done justice to the Indians. The process of change has been pursued too rapidly. Great difficulties attend the disestablishment of the reservation system... *In general, it might be stated that the policy of the United States in dealing with American Indians contain little that can be followed in governing the backward races here* (Italics mine—V.B.L.)[6]

In particular, Barrows proposed that the reservation system be avoided in dealing with the minority, and that "the government should not cede or grant any public land to a tribe as a tribe." He advocated isolation as a policy for the Negritos for a certain length of time, but believed that for the Mangyans and other tribes of "Malayan origin, on a lower cultural plane than the Christian Filipino...governmental efforts should tend to encourage admixture rather than to maintain isolation."[7]

He reasoned that these tribes had advanced to the point of understanding individual ownership of property. Yet, a closer look at the proposition would indicate a utilitarian end, as the assignment of individual land holdings itself would leave superfluous land open to settlement from the outside. As conceived, the goal was toward a peaceful coexistence of the majority and the minority groups, with regard to the use of land areas.

Barrows further proposed on the basis of his examination of Indian education in the U.S. that the immediate objectives which education should pursue among the tribes here should be the teaching of English coupled with reading and writing. He likewise recommended the establishment of boarding industrial schools to be planted in each major tribe and administered by the Americans.

[6] *Ibid.*, p. 684.
[7] *Ibid.*

On the other hand, Barrows strongly argued against entrusting police and judicial authority on any ethnic group—whether "Filipino Christian or non-Christian." Contrasting Indian society and the "Malayan society" in the Philippines, he asserted that while the former was thoroughly democratic, the latter was

> ...oppressively aristocratic. The power of the man of wealth, position, or inheritance is inordinate. He is not only able to commit abuses, but is morally blinded to their enormity. Beneath him the man of poverty and unenlightened mind takes rank with animals that till the soil. I believe that this characterization is true of both Christian and non-Christian communities. The entrusting of authority, then... should be safeguarded and restricted in every possible way.[8]

Contrary to what Leothiny Clavel and Mamintal Tamano believe,[9] the Bureau of Non-Christian Tribes did not continually function up to the Commonwealth Period.[10] It was changed to the Ethnological Survey of the Philippines barely two years after its foundation. While this revised set-up closely approximated the Bureau of American Ethnology which dealt directly with the study of diverse Indian tribes, the results of its work, as Merton Miller said, were only of scientific value, great though this was. The problem of dealing with the tribes in the Philippines was in fact considered "much more important than was the problem in America." Aware that the Americans could never become a majority in the Philippines, Miller called for a careful investigation of American policies concerning the "tribes." "In these respects," he said, "the problem here differs from that which we had to solve in the United States, and from these facts, too, its relatively greater importance appears."[11] Concerning the work of the re-organized bureau, Miller reiterated the plain proposition that the more you knew about a given people the better you could get along with them. The

---

[8] *Ibid.*, p. 685.
[9] Cf. Mamintal A. Tamano, *Needed: A Total Commitment, A Compilation of Writing* (Manila: Bureau of Printing, 1968), pp. 17-18; and Leothiny Clavel, "National Integration: A Case of Planned Change," *Journal on National Integration*, Vol. 1, No. 1 (Quezon City, 1968), pp. 19, 32.
[10] In truth, Dean C. Worcester reported in 1903 that the Bureau of Non-Christian Tribe was changed to "Ethnological Survey for the Philippine Islands" (cf. "Report of the Secretary of the Interior," *Fourth Annual Report of the Philippine Commission*, 1903, Part 2 (Washington: Government Printing Office, 1904), p. 789.
[11] *Fourth Annual Report of the Philippine Commission, op. cit.*

agency was conceived as practically useful "in the work of controlling and assisting in their progress the uncivilized people in the island."[12]

However, the actual task of governing the minority groups from the onset of American rule up to 1916 fell directly under the office of the Secretary of the Interior. As such, Worcester, who was the Secretary of the Interior until 1913, exercised executive control over the affairs of all members of non-Christian tribes outside the "Moro province." Likewise, he had the power to approve executive orders and memoranda which once promulgated had the force of law for the minority groups.

For instance, Worcester drafted and authored the so-called "Special Provincial Government Act" (Act No. 1396, Sept. 4, 1905) promulgated by the Philippine Commission of which he was also a member. This act directly affected the lives of the non-Christian groups as it provided for the organization and administration of the "special provinces" inhabited by the minority groups. Prior to the passage of this law, Mindoro itself was detached from Marinduque Province and given a provincial government of its own by Act No. 500 (Nov. 10, 1902) of the Philippine Commission.[13] In particular, Section 18 of the same act authorized the governor of Mindoro, subject to the approval of the Secretary of Interior, to deal with and provide for the government of the Mangyans.

The diverse roles the governor assumed in his post hindered him from doing full-time work among the Mangyans. Thus, efforts made to uplift Mangyan life were limited to the establishment of settlements which covered only a small sector of the Mangyan population. It must be added that settlements were established in spite of Barrows' prior recommendations against transplanting the reservation system into the country.

The set-up in the settlement established in Mindoro was a miniature form of the municipal government at that time. In effect,

> A presidente and "consejal" were appointed, but no attempt was made to organize any form of township government. Orders were given these officials to keep the place clean, plant anything they saw fit, and to encourage others to join them.
>
> The regular form of municipal appointment was given the presidente, to which was added brightly colored seals and ribbons, and it would be

[12] *Ibid.*
[13] See *Report of the Philippine Commission*, Vol. 11, Part 1, *op. cit.*, p. 542.

a matter to attach as much importance to his position as do these savages.[14]

In brief, the Americans established a form of government for the Mangyans which entailed a chain of command from the governor to the elected lowlanders who supervised Mangyan affairs. The Mangyans were not given a chance to govern themselves. Often, they were governed by Filipinos who in many cases were the major sources of abuses. As Offley himself reported, the biggest rascal in the community was often the elected *presidente,* who owed his power to the fear the people had of him.

By and large, the efforts of the Americans to organize Mangyan settlements turned out to be a total failure. The nomadic character of majority of the Mangyans as well as the absence of tribal relations were seen as major barriers to the success of U.S. policies concerning them. As Offley lamented, "Each family is mortally afraid of the other, which makes progress with them exceedingly slow."[15] It may be added that the attendant use of sheriff force in the establishment of such villages as well as the oppressive rule of the lowland presidentes made it doubly difficult for the Mangyans to trust the sincerity of the colonial masters. Worcester, the author of this scheme, blamed the failure of the settlement system on the attitude of "Tagalog Filipinos" who, according to him,

> ... look with great disfavor on the gathering of the Mangyans into settlements where they can be protected, as it renders it difficult to hold them in a state of peonage. Whenever Gen. Offley got a little group together they did their best to scatter it.[16]

Notwithstanding Worcester's claim, the accounts of this period clearly show that the Americans were themselves exploiters of the Mangyans. Paul Schebesta, a German anthropologist who visited one of the settlements, noted how the Mangyans were cultivating abaca[17]—a sign that they were to some extent integrated into the agro-commercial world system prevailing at that time. In point of fact, Offley himself revealed how one Mangyan settlement named Lalauigan produced a good crop for the fiscal year 1904. For that year, he reported that

---

[14] *Ibid.*
[15] *Ibid.*
[16] D.C. Worcester, *The Philippine Past and Present, op. cit.,* p. 464.
[17] Paul Schebesta, *Menschen Ohne Geschichte* (St. Gabriel-Modling, 1935), p. 135, translated by Dr. Zeus A. Salazar.

> A good crop of corn and camotes was raised and cocoanut (sic) and hemp planted, and I am now requested to furnish them cans in which they can gather rubber. Mr. Manguian is not at all backward about asking what he wants. Requests for carabao, plow, and seeds are frequent...[18]

An outsider's view of the American scheme for the Mangyan development program is further provided by Schebesta. Speaking of the role of his informant, Kaig, in the American administration of Mangyan affairs, Schebesta wrote, that

> For a certain length of time, Kaig played the role of superintendent among the savage Mangyans. At that time, when the American government went about in a hyperphilanthropic way to build model schools among the Mangyans, Kaig was given the responsibility of overseeing the Mangyans in the north of the land. Kaig knew and fulfilled the responsibility given him. The enterprise which was extraordinarily expensive was in no way related, however, to the results which it showed. Kaig himself had a very pessimistic opinion of it; he was convinced that the desired goal could not be reached with the paid civil forces or servants...[19]

A growing demand that the administration of the non-Christian groups be turned over to the Filipinos caused the American civil government to re-examine their policies toward the minority groups in 1909. Worcester in his annual report noted how the demand "has been made so publicly and so persistently as practically to force its consideration."[20] In defense of the *status quo,* Worcester reiterated the oft-repeated point made by the Americans in justification of their policy—the question of the Filipinos'

> ability and fitness to dominate, justly control, and wisely guide along the pathway of civilization alien people... (i.e., the non-Christian tribes)[21]

Worcester argued on three major points to support his trenchant words against the Filipino demand for government of the non-Christian tribes: first, there existed a wide cultural gap between the Filipino and the minority groups; second, the Filipino had no just claim to ownership of the territory occupied by "wild men"; third, the Filipino was

---

[18] *Report of the Philippine Commission,* Vol. 11, Part 1, *op. cit.*
[19] Paul Schebesta, *op. cit.,* p. 137.
[20] "Report of the Secretary of the Interior" in *Report of the Philippine Commission, 1909-1911* (Washington: Government Printing Office, n.d.), p. 74.
[21] *Ibid.*

TOWARDS THE IDEA OF INTEGRATION 113

ignorant of the hill tribes. "Mutual distrust and hatred" formed, according to the irate colonial master, "an insurmountable barrier between Filipino and non-Christian."

In effect, Worcester's view of majority-minority relations outlined the United States' policy on the ethnic problems in this period. As Secretary of the Interior, Worcester decided the tenor of the U.S. attitude toward the minorities, which at this stage favored isolation rather than admixture of pagans, Muslims and Christians. In his annual report to the Philippine Commission (1910), Worcester expressed the opinion that

> ... to turn the control of the non-Christian tribes over to the Filipinos would speedily result in disaster. As the Filipinos have no just claim to the territory which the non-Christians occupy, I see no reason for pursuing such a course.[22]

A staunch isolationist, Worcester propounded at length the American view that the "Filipinos" comprised a distinct race and culture from the minorities. His argument was that

> It is true that the Filipino, the Igorot, and the Moro are of common racial origin, but so are the Anglo-Saxon peoples, and there exists between the Filipinos on the one side and Igorots and the Moros on the other, far greater difference than those which distinguish the Germans, the English, and the Americans. Indeed, the width of the gap between the Filipino, whose Malayan blood has been profoundly modified by intermarriage with people of other races, and who has attained to a degree of civilization far above that ever reached by any other Malayan people, and the wild man of the Luzon mountains, with his pure blood, his magnificent physical development, and his primitive customs and instincts, is very great...[23]

Ironically, merely a year after Worcester's solid pronouncement on Filipino non-Christian "diversity," the Philippine Bill of 1913 was passed, providing for extended powers of self-government to the Filipinos. This, of course, also effected a radical change in the U.S. policy concerning the majority-minority relations. The change in the policy was in fact defined in the 1914 report of the acting governor-general. Significantly, the new policy provided answers to the issues raised by Worcester, who by then had resigned from his post as Secretary of the Interior. In part, the report stated that

[22] Ibid., p. 81.
[23] Ibid., p. 75.

> By this policy the isolation in which the mountain people were left for so many generations will gradually be removed and the way opened for a more rapid spread of civilization. By this means also, the distrust heretofore reported to exist between the hill people and the civilized people of the plains will be eliminated and a feeling of mutual regard and respect will be engendered. *It is obvious that common feelings of nationality among the peoples of the Philippines can only be secured by bringing them into association and contact with each other. Maintaining and strengthening the barrier which has in the past been erected between them will not serve* (Italics mine—V.B.L.).[24]

The idea of a common nationality, engendered by the propagandists and finding its most intense expression in the Revolution of 1896, reached at this point a form so distinct and vivid as to force the Americans to come to grips with it. Thus, in the "Moro country," as well as in the Mt. Province, a new policy was inaugurated of "cultivating confidence and goodwill between the non-Christians and their Christian neighbors." In Mindoro, however, the death of Mr. Jesse D. David, the assigned Mangyan agent, momentarily hindered change of policy.

Changes were also made to centralize the work of the Department of Interior among the non-Christians. Winfred T. Dennison, the successor of Worcester, introduced a bill in the Philippine Commission which placed the administration of the non-Christians in the charge of a new officer, known as "Delegate of the Secretary of the Interior for the non-Christian people." However, direct supervision of the tribes was increasingly delegated to the provincial and municipal governments.

The apparent failure of the new system, as well as the general disorganization of the work among the minority groups, led to the reconstitution of the defunct Bureau of Non-Christian Tribes in 1917. The underlying principle in its reorganization was the advancement of what the Americans characteristically described as "backward elements of the population" to economic, political and social equality and unification with the majority group. The law creating it gave it the duty:

> ...to continue the work for advancement and liberty in favor of the regions inhabited by non-Christian Filipinos and to foster by all adequate means and in a systematic, rapid and complete manner the moral, material, economic, social and political development of those regions

---

[24] "Report of the Governor-General" in *Report of the Philippine Commission to the Secretary of War* (Washington: Government Printing Office, 1915), p. 39.

always having in view the aim of rendering permanent the mutual intelligence between and complete fusion of all the Christian and non-Christian elements populating the Provinces of the Archipelago....²⁵

The newly defined goals of the bureau constituted a clear departure from what it formerly stood for—an arm for tribal research and a policy-making body for the minorities. In a word, the bureau was revived to work for the eventual assimilation of all tribal groups into the mainstream of the national life. As the Governor-General stated in his report of 1917, the final objective

... is obviously the eventual discontinuance of the bureau of non-Christian tribes by the passing of its territory to the jurisdiction of the executive bureau as regularly organized provincial territory as rapidly as the people by advance in civilization shall have qualified for such autonomous provincial and local government...²⁶

For the first time, too, the supervision and administration of the work in Mindanao and Sulu were integrated into the totality of government programs for the minority groups. The Department of Mindanao and Sulu was thus abolished and the domain of the newly reconstituted bureau expanded to include the special provinces of Agusan, Bukidnon, Cotabato, Davao, Lanao, Mt. Province, Nueva Vizcaya, Sulu and Zamboanga. Obviously, Mindoro was not classified as a special province. This was presumably because the Mangyans, unlike the Muslims and the Mt. Province tribes, did not constitute a political voice nor a threat to the security of the colonial government. On the other hand, the areas listed as special provinces (where most of the non-Christian funds went) were all troubled areas—that is, the scene of armed conflicts and bitter struggles. Thus, the Muslims and the ethnic groups from the Mt. Province and Nueva Vizcaya were the sole groups which truly benefited from the positive measures taken by the colonial government.

In the formulation of policies toward the non-Christians then, the Mangyans likewise suffered discrimination in the hands of the Americans. For instance, the Supreme Court stand regarding Mangyan civil rights which figured in a court case in 1926, defined that the "Manguianes are not free as civilized men are free."²⁷ Though a

---
²⁵ *Report of the Governor-General of the Philippines to the Secretary of War,* 1917 (Washington: Government Printing Office, 1918), p. 29.
²⁶ *Ibid.*
²⁷ Edmond Block and H. L. Noble, *op. cit.*

"person within the meaning of the habeas corpus law," the Mangyan was not considered the equal of his lowland brother. This policy, of course, further aggravated the distinction between the lowlanders and the Mangyans.

In the '20s, the influx of migrants from other regions as a result of the incentives given by the colonial government led to the intensification of the growing land problems in Mindoro. To cope with these conflicts posed by "Christian landgrabbers," Mindoro was included among the special provinces supervised by the Bureau of Non-Christian Tribes. This change in the policy prescribed that the bureau, through the provincial governor, should henceforth exercise control and supervision over the territory occupied by the Mangyans. Steps were also taken to reserve the lands inhabited by the Mangyans, but this effort, as may be inferred from the reports, was not extensively carried out.

An over-all change in the American policy toward the minorities is apparent with the beginning of a new era in Philippine history in the '30s. At this point, the embryonic concept of a total national community acquired a more definite form which, in turn, paved the way for the creation of the concept of integration. One of the first acts passed in the inaugural session of the "First National Assembly" under the Commonwealth was one which abolished the Bureau of Non-Christian Tribes. This action is significant as it showed the keen desire of the pioneer Filipino lawmakers to foster national unity and solidarity by abolishing any trace of distinctions set between "Christians and non-Christians." The whole tenor of the Filipino policy toward the minorities in fact centered around the idea of integration. Justifying the act, the late President Manuel Luis Quezon declared before the First National Assembly that there was no longer a need for the continued existence of "specialized rule" for the minorities of Luzon, including Mindoro and Palawan "whatever may have been the reason for instituting this arrangement." He further stated,

> ... they today no longer exist to an extent sufficient to justify the continuation of the Bureau of Non-Christian Tribes. Considering the marked advancement in the civilization and general progress of the special provinces, the so-called non-Christian problem has been reduced to one of solidification and development and our present efforts are directed towards the simplification of the government agencies so as to insure efficiency.[28]

[28] *Message of the President,* Vol. 2, Part 1, Revised Edition (Manila: Bureau of Printing, 1938), p. 200.

Under the Commonwealth government, then, the task of administering the minority groups was assigned to the Department of Interior, "insuring a better coordination of the development work that may be authorized by the national government for said region."[29] Recognizing the difficulty of integrating the Muslims in the South, the Commonwealth government created the Office of the Commissioner for Mindanao and Sulu to direct the development work for the said area. This office continued to function until the outbreak of the Pacific war in 1941.

The brevity of the Japanese occupation of the Philippines did not leave any indelible mark on the Mangyans of Mindoro. Conklin, for instance, mentioned in an article written shortly after the war that the Hanunoo had virtually no contact with either Japanese or American troops during the Occupation. "When an occasional dogfight took place over their territory," he reported, "they ran to the family burial caves for safety and to be near their ancestors."[30] Except for this reference in Conklin's work, there seems to be no other existing account of Mangyan life during the Second World War. Macario Landicho wrote of mass evacuations into the interior as a consequence of the Japanese occupation of Mindoro,[31] but he made no reference to the Mangyans. One is left then merely to suppose that in this new movement inland of coastal residents, reminiscent of the days of piracy when the same thing happened, the Mangyans were again pushed further into the depths of Mt. Halcon.

The end of the war brought to the fore the existing undercurrents in Muslim-Christian relations in Mindanao and Sulu. In the early '50s this broke out into armed conflicts between the government forces and 'Moro bandits'—a fact which further underscored the age-old problem of Muslim integration into the national community. To resolve this major threat to the peaceful co-existence of Muslims and Christians in the region, a congressional committee was formed in 1954 to investigate the problem. The findings of the Committee revealed that the problem had deeply-rooted sources, transcending the question of "peace and order" in the South. It was found out that the problem

---

[29] *Op. cit.*
[30] Harold C. Conklin, "Bamboo Literacy in Mindoro," *Pacific Discovery*, Vol. 2, No. 4 (July-August 1949), p. 7.
[31] Macario Landicho, *op. cit.*, p. 79.

had assumed historic, economic, social, educational and political significance.

One of the primary achievements of the committee was the creation of a Commission charged with the specific mission to enhance the progress of the Muslims and the other minority groups. Specifically, the law creating the Commission on National Integration (R.A. 1888) on June 22, 1957, declared that henceforth the government's policy toward the minorities was

> To effectuate in a more rapid and complete manner the economic, social, moral and political advancement of the non-Christian Filipinos or national cultural minorities and to render real, complete and permanent the integration of all said national cultural communities into the body politic...[32]

Among the more important functions of the newly-created Commission as specified in section four of the said law were the following:

(a) To engage in industrial and agricultural enterprises and establish processing plants and cottage industries to lead communities of national cultural communities in engaging such pursuits and, upon the attainment of this objective, to sell such enterprises or industries to them at cost.

(b) To construct, operate and maintain irrigation systems and dams, power structures or generating plants, electric transmission and distribution lines or systems for the furnishing of electric light, heat and power to the inhabitants in the areas not receiving the service of such plants or systems.

(c) To cooperate with government agricultural experimental stations or demonstration farms (*sic*) and agricultural supervisors in assisting farmers to acquire knowledge of modern farming or better methods of cultivation of farms.

(d) To effectuate the settlement of all the landless members of the National Cultural Minorities by procuring homesteads for them or by resettling them in resettlement projects of the National Resettlement and Rehabilitation Administration.

(e) To cause the establishment of more public schools in regions inhabited by the National Cultural Minorities and encourage them to attend the same.

(f) To assist in the training of the National Cultural Minorities in the different fields of education and to help them secure employment in private establishments or offices in the civil service.

---

[32] From the true copy of Republic Act No. 1888 (As amended by Republic Act No. 3852, 1973 Constitution, P.D. No. 193), p. 1.

(g) To authorize lawyers of the Commission to assist indigent members of the cultural minorities accused in criminal cases involving their landholdings.[33]

While the work of the CNI appears impressive in print, its actual performance among the Mangyans in Mindoro does not appear equally laudable. Since its inception in 1957, no breakthrough has been made in the total integration of the Mangyans into the national community. Hitherto, only one Mangyan settlement could be rightfully said to have received regular assistance from the CNI.[34] As a matter of fact, work and rehabilitation programs in Mindoro have been for the most part, uncoordinated. The Social Welfare Administration, missions and private social action groups continue to do their work individually. No effort has been made by the CNI to integrate these and other existing Mangyan welfare programs. Thus, development work among the Mangyans is largely *laissez-faire* in character—each "social action" group is left to interpret what is best for the Mangyans they are dealing with. Of course, not all civic-conscious groups come up with positive programs for change. The SWA, which initiated social welfare work among the Irayas in Bayanan, Mayabig, has encouraged dependency on aids and dole-outs rather than encouraging self-sufficiency among the villagers.[35]

As defined by law, the CNI was to serve as the government's arm for national integration. While this concept acquired greater prominence in recent years, its operations have been confined mainly to the majority group among the minorities. The Muslims, being large in number and constituting a political force, have received considerable attention from the government. On account perhaps of their generally passive and withdrawing character, the Mangyans have never been accorded the same or even remotely similar assistance and support.

[33] *Ibid.*, p. 2.
[34] This is one Buhid settlement located in Batangan, Bongabon. Development work among the Hanunoo was initiated by Fr. Antoon Postma and recently supplemented by independent projects undertaken by the Mangyan Integrated Development Program and the Elizalde group, Panamin. Welfare work among the northern groups has been very minimal—only those living in the foothills have received occasional help from the SWA and Catholic and Protestant missionary groups.
[35] The SWA's welfare project in Bayanan, Mayabig, is sporadic in nature— no long-range project has been instituted and the continuance of the work relies heavily on the commitment of the individual social worker assigned in the area. Several attempts were made to introduce cottage industries but this did not last long as the Irayas were more concerned with their *kaingins* which provide them a sure source of food.

To make matters worse, the government agents sent to work among the Mangyans, in a number of instances, have been the source of fraud and treachery themselves. The first CNI representative to the Mangyans (a Kalinga man and thus, a member of a cultural community himself) did not only swindle hundreds of Mangyans of their small earnings, but likewise illegally had reservation lands surveyed and sold to lowlanders.[36] It was only with the concerted action of Mangyans and missionaries that this man was relieved of his post. In other cases, municipal officials themselves took advantage of the Mangyans' ignorance in the ways of lowland culture by overcharging them in the payment of their taxes and other governmental fees.[37] All this is quite discouraging to the Mangyans who are eager to do everything, even pay taxes and fill up all sorts of bureaucratic forms, just to secure titles for their lands before avaricious lowlanders take over them.

Though the present government policy theoretically provides for opportunity and freedom for the Mangyans and other minority groups to preserve their cultural identity, the onslaughts of lowland pressures and the undirected (and, sometimes, misdirected) introduction of changes have led some Mangyan groups into social dysphoria. Unless the government takes a more active part in meaningful projects for these people, the continuous influx of lowlanders and their modernizing influences may soon bring an end to a culture which is of immense importance to our understanding of our history as a people.

---

[36] Cf. Caroline Stickley, *op. cit.*, p. 193. Interviews were also made both with O.M.F. missionaries, and Mangyans who were involved in this case.

[37] In Pinamalayan and Batangan, Bongabon, some Mangyans were made to pay as high as ₱150.00 for their income taxes. Considering the meager income the Mangyans make out of their *kaingins*, the fee is really unreasonable.

CHAPTER SIX

Summary and
Conclusion

IT WAS pointed out at the outset that the object of this study is to provide a historical view of the Mangyan problem. The goal was to provide a perspective other than what has been given by anthropologists or missionaries. For one cannot truly know and understand a people apart from its historical experience. Moreover, the diachronic view of the Mangyans, the historical substance inferred from voluminous documentary materials should complement what has been achieved so far in Mangyan studies.

The long history of the Mangyans brings us as far back as the much longer pre-Spanish era. While this period has not been totally unveiled, there is ample evidence to support the statement that the Mangyan is an "ancient man." In fact, we could say with certainty that the progenitors of the Mangyans were among the first Filipinos to develop ties with the Asian world. The bulk of archaeological finds that have been uncovered in Mindoro, together with a number of references in Chinese dynastic accounts, points to the existence of thriving settlements in the island's coastal areas long before the coming of the Spaniards. Though the ties with China and other Asian countries were tenuous, this early form of culture contact in Mindoro was contributory to the development of a rich pre-Hispanic culture in Mindoro.

At the point of contact with Spain, the Spaniards found Mindoro an island of relative importance. Contrary to what one writer believes,[1] the impression given in the accounts of the pioneer expedition to Mindoro (and a number of other documentary materials) is not of a "sparsely populated island" and an "unexplored wilderness." The accounts speak rather of maritime towns or "pueblos," and fortifications 14 feet thick with moats. The coastal people, on the other hand, were depicted as possessing a relatively advanced culture—they were elaborate in manner of dressing, and had a diverse collection of arms which was made possible through a relatively advanced knowledge of metallurgy. The natives were also described as using gold, a fact which the Spaniards readily tapped for their own ends. In addition, references made to the Spanish encounter with a number of Chinese junks carrying native products and exchange goods certainly negates Echevarria's point that Mindoro had never been commercially important in historic times.[2]

Found along the direction of Spanish colonial expansion, Mindoro became a colony of Spain in 1570 after a weak armed resistance made by natives living along the coasts. Accompanied by the now classic symbols of the Cross and the Sword, the Spaniards effected radical changes in the lives of the Mindoro natives. The social order was restructured, turning an independent people into vassals of Spain. Yet not all islanders accepted the new colonial power. Some refused to remain under the sphere of Spanish influence and withdrew, finding refuge in the interior. This initial response to colonial pressure is of

---

[1] Cf. Ramon Echevarria, *Rediscovery in Southern Cebu* (Cebu City: Barba Press, 1974), p. 66. Echevarria also tries to make a case for Cebu's being the ancient Ma-yi mentioned in the account of Chao-Ju-Kua and other Chinese chroniclers. His argument, however, is based principally on the extensive prosperity of Cebu at contact point with Spain (due principally to trade with China) on the one hand and on the lack of population and prosperity of Mindoro in recent years. The latter island was of course one of the more populated and prosperous regions in the Philippines when the Spaniards came. It was the so-called "Moro Wars" which contributed to the depletion of its population. Furthermore, the amount of porcelain and other trade wares continually being unearthed and showing up in Mindoro would tend to make this island one of the principal areas of porcelain finds in our country, despite the lack of any systematic excavations thus far.

[2] *Ibid. passim*. In fact, when Legaspi established the Spanish settlement in Cebu, there was hardly any report of Chinese in the environs (cf. Andrew Sharp, *Adventurous Armada the Story of Legaspi's Expedition*) (Christchurch, New Zealand: Whitcombe and Tombs, Ltd., 1961), pp. 94 *et seq*. and also the volumes in B & R referring to the Legaspi Expedition.

import, for the process of withdrawal out of the sphere of Spanish control later led to diverse differentiation of cultures between those who decided to remain in the lowland area on the one hand, and those who opted to flee into the highlands of Mindoro on the other hand. Undoubtedly, those who remained within the pale of Spanish control embraced the Catholic faith and consequently absorbed, though selectively, Spanish cultural practices. This process of Hispanization was, of course, the fruit of determined religious evangelization that started alongside the pacification of the island from 1570 onwards. This compelling influence of the religious clerics led to differentiation between "infieles" and believers, later perceived as the Mangyan-Lowland Christian dichotomy during the American colonial regime.

The compelling religious influence exerted by the pioneer Spanish missionaries thus formed one of the earliest pressures on Mangyan life. However, this religious strain should not be set apart from the concomitant pressure exerted by the colonial government. The flourishing island, known for its excellent port and thriving pueblos underwent rapid deterioration with the *degagé* manner of colonial administration. This was exacerbated by the onslaughts of piratical attacks—which, in themselves, constituted a form of response to Spain's encroachment on Muslim territories.

Owing to its excellent harbors and numerous coves, Mindoro became a convenient base for "Moro" piratical operations which became another source of pressure on the natives of Mindoro. The three centuries of Muslim piratical activity in Mindoro was undeniably a tremendous constraint on the lives of its indigenous people. Taken as captives and sold as slaves, at times killed without mercy, the natives were indeed innocent pawns caught in the contest between Spanish and Muslim supremacy in the region. While one admires the bravery and defiant character of the Muslim response to Spanish rule, the natives of Mindoro and not the Spaniards were the ones who, in the final analysis, truly bore the brunt of Muslim assaults. Moreover, the consistent burning of towns, either by the "Moro" pirates or the rampaging Spanish, the ransacking of homes and capture of natives for the slave market, could very well have brought Mindoro to its end as an island of major importance. A further effect must have been to drive the population either into exile in safer places or to send them inland to comparative safety, disrupting the development of well-established settlements along the coasts.

The combined piratical and colonial pressures brought an end to the former florescence of the island, a fact which has become mythical to many who are ignorant of the rich, historic past of Mindoro. Alongside the disastrous effect of Muslim piracy, the Spanish exaction of heavy tributes, the imposition of burdensome monopolies, and the unreasonable demand for forced labor left the island largely depopulated and its inhabitants greatly impoverished. A further and more significant consequence was the intermingling and inevitable "cross-ethnic" relations in the interior. These "cross-ethnic" relations brought about by the now classic response of "withdrawal" reflected in the oft-repeated inland movement in times of stress, seem to have largely contributed to the growth of ethnic multiplicity among the interior people. The sources that have been surveyed appear to allow the inference that the "Mangyans" may have constituted themselves as groups in response to the pressures from the outside. As a matter of fact, the culture of the present Mangyan groups seems to show retained elements of the ancient Bisayan culture.[3]

At the close of the 19th century, we find the term "Mangyans" used collectively to denote a diverse set of people. Better knowledge of these interior people made possible by concerned religious workers and pioneering Mangyan researchers like de Zuñiga, Jordana, and Blumentritt provides a substantial picture of a people significantly different from the Hispanized lowland group. The influx of natives from other islands as a result of the Spanish attempts at reviving the former prosperity of Mindoro led to the swelling of the lowland Christian population. Towards the end of the Spanish rule, the isolated groups in the interior emerged as the minority in the island of Mindoro. Yet, while we speak of a minority people, the issue of integration at this point was still in its germinal stage. This was so, because, until the Revolution, the concept of national community would not come into fruition, and it would only be such a socio-political totality that could invoke the idea of integration. Only the existence of a Filipino national aspiration and of a state fundamentally different from the hierarchic

---

[3] Cf. Alzina, *Historia de Bisaya*, who mentions the *ambahan*, and other cultural elements we know as "Mangyans" and also Chirino, *Relacion de las Islas Filipinas*.

Spanish colonial system would make the idea of integration relevant in terms of the union of all indigenous groups in the Philippines.

Though we speak of social distance between Mangyans and lowlanders in this period, a limited form of social contact existed which was primarily exploitative in nature. In fact, the Mangyans were actually assimilated into the worldwide capitalist system through various chains whose closest links to the Mangyans were the lowlanders and their Spanish colonial masters. This exploitative character of lowland-Mangyan relations which were laid down during the Spanish colonial regime intensified with the coming of the Americans and, unfortunately, perpetuated up to our day.

The concept of a "minority" became increasingly manifest in Mindoro as a new and stronger colonial force took over the effete Spanish rulers. For one thing, the Americans took an active hand in the administration of tribal peoples. The concept of "non-Christian" tribes adopted and adapted from their predecessors was fostered by the creation of special colonial agencies for the Mangyans and by efforts to restructure these into Indian-like reservations. These moves, of course, aggravated the tribal people's position as a group distinct from the Filipinos—that is, the civilized Christian lowland group.

Notwithstanding the Americans' divisive view of the Christian-non-Christian Filipinos, a number of American field researchers brought to the fore a better knowledge of the Mangyans' ethnic groupings. Starting with the crude and dubious naturalistic explorations which treated the Mangyans as mere objects of curiosity, Mangyan studies progressively moved to more scientific studies in the 20th century. Thus, though the term "Mangyan" has a long history of usage, it was only in this age that the people known by this appellation became more accurately identified. Indeed, the knowledge of the different Mangyan groups today bears greater accuracy and substance than a century ago.

In spite of this determination of ethnic divisions, the various Mangyan groups were still considered as a totality in relation to the dominant lowland Christian groups. Their relations to the Filipino community as a whole were determined and circumscribed in various ways by lawmakers in different periods. These policies ranged from "isolation" in the early part of the American rule through the modified concept of "admixture," and consequently, to that of "integration" under the

Commonwealth and the Republic. The idea of integration, of course, was a consequence of the perception of nationality engendered late in the 19th century and brought into fruition with the final attainment of freedom.

However, the road leading to Mangyan integration was fraught with obstacles. These obstacles took the form of pressures, both old and new. The old pressures were shown to have been institutionalized under the American colonial rule, and perpetuated even under the present dispensation. In our own times, pressures on land, property and even life itself, comprise the new forces that impinge on Mangyan life. These pressures come from land-obsessed migrants who may have been displaced themselves or impelled to move into Mangyan land by the sheer desire to amass wealth.

Positive governmental action is virtually unknown to the Mangyans. The little work that the defunct CNI undertook among the Buhid Mangyans is not even worthy of mention. The CNI representatives sent to work in Mindoro will surely be remembered by the Mangyans, not as agents of good but of exploitation. To this day, there is no programmed strategy for development work among the minority groups in Mindoro. Welfare work is done at random by various groups with each having its own philosophy of effecting change among these communities. Consequently, the Mangyans are flung headlong into unchartered paths of modernization.

Like many tribal groups in the throes of modernization, the Mangyans face the threat of extinction. It is truly ironic that they who have been able to preserve indigenous Filipino culture through centuries of foreign rule, should now give way to the compelling forces brought to bear on them by their own Westernized Filipino kindred. While we speak of "cultural communities" instead of "cultural minorities" in our day, and while the government rejects the idea of majority-minority differentiation among the members of the national community, the fact remains that the Mangyans and other traditional groups still live apart and away from the dominant Christian Filipinos.

Almost two decades have passed since the Philippine Republic vowed to "effectuate in a more rapid and complete manner the economic, social, moral, and political advancement" of the national cultural minorities, and "to render real, complete and permanent the integration" of such groups into the national body politic. The CNI, created

SUMMARY AND CONCLUSION 127

as an arm to effect this policy, has come and gone; yet the Mangyans still have to see the day when such a generous vision will have been fulfilled. Meanwhile, the Mangyans on their own volition have opted to respond to changes by joining barangays and the *Samahang Nayon,* paying their taxes and bringing their cases to court, with the hope that in the near future they may be recognized as full-fledged members of the national community. The problem, therefore, is how we may help them achieve this goal. There may actually be two directions for this.

Asked what his utmost ambition in life is, an Iraya Mangyan whom the writer met on one of her field trips readily replied: *"Nais kong maging kagaya ng Tagalog."*

"Like the Tagalogs"—this secret wish mirrors the deep yearnings of a growing number of Mangyans. The reply of the Iraya man from northern Mindoro signifies not only a whimsical desire to be dressed like his lowland kin, or to talk like him—it represents a deeper longing to become like the Tagalogs in terms of enjoying the same rights, privileges and opportunities, of being recognized and accepted within the total Philippine community.

What shall then be the place of Mangyans in the Filipino national community? The Mangyan's wish cited above provides one clue to a probable mode of Mangyan integration—that is, a live option to become assimilated into the dominant lowland Tagalog culture. This approach seems to be a more realistic alternative, given the existing conditions in majority-minority relations in Mindoro today.

The idealists may scoff at the idea and protest that this view will mean the total loss of the aboriginal Mangyan cultures, but the reality is that it may no longer be possible to preserve the indigenous Mangyan cultures in their pristine form. In truth, there exists no Mangyan group today that has not been exposed to nor encroached upon by people coming from the lowlands—missionaries, land-grabbers, anthropologists, social workers, lumberjacks have long penetrated and disrupted the continuity of traditional way of life. Willingly or unwillingly, the overwhelming external pressures have transformed a significant number of Mangyans into nondescript "types." Nowadays, it is not uncommon to see an Iraya man dressed in gaudy lowland clothes, smoking cigarettes, drinking alcohol and cursing in Tagalog. Faced with these realities, a government-directed acculturation and assimilation of the northern Mangyan groups into the dominant and relatively "acceptable" Tagalog culture may prove to be more realistic.

Among the Hanunoo and Buhids, a more fitting approach would probably be one which recognizes their ethnic identity and even welcomes it as a contribution to the rich variety of the Filipino national heritage. The Hanunoo and Buhid *ambahans,* their ancient Indic script, the still thriving weaving industry and pottery-making, the intricate rituals of death and birth, not only provide a window to our pre-Hispanic past but undoubtedly also form a potential contribution to the patterning of the evolving Filipino culture.

While the two alternatives for Mangyan integration vary in form, they will eventually converge as Pilipino becomes established as a lingua franca among them. The use of Pilipino as a medium of communication in their dealings with the lowlanders in public schools and barangay meetings will eventually tend towards the unification not only of Mangyan cultures but more so of Filipino culture as a whole. The workability of this ideal may be inferred from the already established use of Filipino as a channel for communication in Mangyan inter-"tribal" conferences and the Mangyan Bible School, jointly organized by believers from the different Mangyan tribes and the O.M.F. missionaries. The difficulties of cross-ethnic communication have been minimized by the introduction of Pilipino as a means of communication among ethnic groups speaking different dialects.

Beyond the integration of the Mangyans, the study of their rich cultural heritage should be pushed further, if only to provide a broader and more human basis for understanding them and ourselves as a nation. As this book hopefully shows, the Mangyans do not merely constitute an area for anthropological or religious studies. The rich, historical past of the Mangyans equally provides a challenging and relevant field for research.

The historical study of the Mangyans is feasible because there are manifold existing source materials. In fact, documentary, archaeological and ethnographic materials all provide a rich source for problems other than what has been surveyed in this book. One could, for instance, make a cultural inventory of Mangyan culture as compared to the ancient Bisayan culture, as this may still be inferred from extant document materials.

SUMMARY AND CONCLUSION 129

The problems surveyed in this study could likewise be continued along the line of acculturative studies. Such a research could look into the modes of integration conflict in the relationship between the dominant lowland groups and the subordinate Mangyan "tribes." In particular, two or three representative Mangyan groups could be taken as subjects to show the interaction and reaction of northern minority groups to lowland penetration. But this of course entails more intensive field work of long duration among them. It is hoped that this work has provided a preliminary "diachronic" basis for just such a "synchronic" study.

Appendix A

KANDA-AMBAHAN OR SONGS.

Ako bangbon rugrugan
Sihan diadgan sa pint'an.
Ako maanton way man.

Translation.
Permit that I be given to eat (or scattered grains of rice)
Like a guest at your door,
And I will give thanks indeed (or given a rice granary).
The play on words in this is quite plain even in the translation.

Si manók si bidláwan,
Ud madí gihitan,
Bakang-kisab kundyan,
Gatlay man sakablitan,
Bida sa ulang kóg'aan.

Translation.
The honey eater bird,
Not yet having left the nest,
A blinking trembler,
Began to be tempted
By a pretty deer,
In the ulang bushes of the cogon meadow.

Anyag di-bay bilogan
Anyag di dua kumahan
Ho hawan bábaye lingban
Iskan kisab sogotan
Kang boyong pang-oopan
Babawo mak ti sindongan.

Translation.
Though I love your body,
I love not to intrude on two.
If one accompany a married woman,
Who shall obey his wink,
His head shall have nightmare
Above in the mountains.

The lex talionis prevails among the Mindoro Mangyans, of whatever tribe, and the penalty for wife stealing is a poisoned arrow some dark night; hence the statement that nightmare shall haunt him above in the mountains is probably correct.

Sample of the Earliest Collection of Hanunoo "Ambahans" from the 1904 Manuscript Collections of Fletcher Gardner.

Appendix B

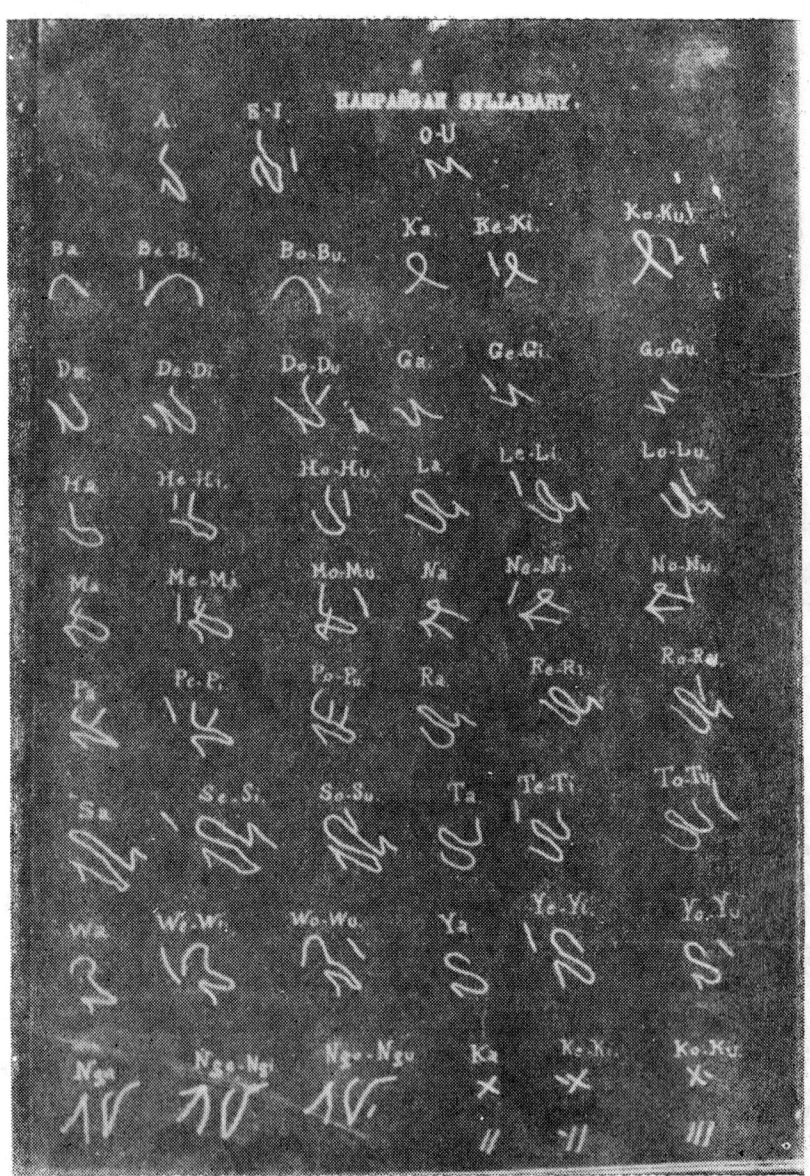

Early Sample of the Mangyan Script Collected by Fletcher Gardner (1904).

Appendix C

Sample of Author's Collection of Buhid Mangyan's "Urukay"

I

Nagtalok ako, ithagay-hagay
Tinmubo sa lanbung balay
Kawdaglantang dagdugay
Mahimanglawun sa balay
Matangisun si Inday

(I planted grass
It sprung forth underneath the house
Please tarry not
For sadness stalks our shack
    and Inday continually cries.)

II

Tan-kagmanok salindunay
Inmuni pudu maangay
Inmapun sa tunga't bugnay
Ang pagkain bigas, abuhay at manok

(The bird and the chicken nestle
    in dry wood,
Continually chirping beautiful notes
Partake of fine, white rice grain.)

III

Gusto ko lamang kag si Inambay sa dalan
Kag managun latay
Sa batang kag managaytay
Pag-uli kaw sa balay kita ga araway
Gaamigos kita anay

(I want Inambay to stay only along the pathway
So we can roam freely in the woods

And when I reach home, you and I
    will not quarrel
And we could remain together.)

IV

Dadi sa balay malaot sing gamay-gamay
Ako ba'y dadi sa balay malaot sing gamay-gamay
Sa batang kagnanagaytay
Sa dalan kagmanagon latay

(I do not wish to stay in the house,
    it's hard for me to bear
I do not wish to stay in the house,
    my mind cannot take it
Among the vine-bridges I will freely cross,
Along the pathway I will roam.)

V

Kahoy-kahoy kot malago
Kabuyong-buyong sing ulo
Kaduyan-duyan sing damgu,
    dalikaw sa pagromedyu
Singhanmu kag sa balay barku
Anay umabut ka nimo

(Like a tree overgrown with branches and leaves,
My mind is full of turmoil
Though loaded with pain and grief
My dreams continually seek for an end,
Let it be known that I am on my way
Perchance you'll catch up with me.)

Bibliography

Books

Agoncillo, Teodoro A. *History of the Filipino People.* Quezon City: Malaya Books, 1967.

Anonymous. "Relacion de las encomiendas existentes en Filipinas." In Wenceslao E. Retana, *Archivo del Bibliofico Filipino.* Madrid, 1898, p. 68.

Anonymous. "Relation of the Voyage to Luzon." Trans. in Emma Helen Blair and James A. Robertson, *The Philippine Islands, 1493-1898.* 55 vols. Cleveland: The Arthur M. Clark Co., 1903-1909.

Arce, Pedro de. "Letter to Philip IV." In E. H. Blair and J. A. Robertson, Vol. 25.

Barham, Marie. *Onak and the Talking Box.* Chicago: Moody Press, 1957.

Barlow, Susanna Morrison. *Mountains Singing.* Chicago: Moody Press, 1960.

Barrantes, Vicente. *Guerras Piraticas de Filipinas Contra Mindanaos Joloanos.* Madrid, 1878, pp. 46-47, 50, 52, 107, 149, 448.

Barreda, V. Monos. "Errores Etnograficos: Los Manguianes de Mindoro." *Oceania Española,* No. 98, 1891.

Beyer, Otley H. "Early History of Philippine Relations with Foreign Countries Especially China." In E. Arsenio Manuel, *Chinese Elements in Tagalog Language.* Manila: 1948, pp. xii, 6.

Block, Edmond and H. Lawrence Noble. *Digest of the Reports of the Supreme Court of the Philippine Islands.* Vol. 4. Rochester, New York: The Lawyers Co-Operative Publishing Company, 1927.

Blount, James H. *The American Occupation of the Philippines, 1898-1912.* New York: G.P. Putnam, 1912.

Careri, Giovanni Francisco Gemelli. "A Voyage to the Philippines." In Awnshamm and John Churchill, *Collection of Voyages and Travels.* London, 1744-1746. Manila: Publications of the Filipiniana Book Guild, Vol. 2, 1963, pp. xi, xxxviii, 29, 33, 42-44, 46, 74, 132-34.

Chirino, Pedro. "Relacion de las islas Filipinas." *Historical Conservation Society,* Vol. 15, 1969, pp. 251, 319.

Colin, Francisco. *Labor Evangelica.* Madrid, 1663. Rep. in 3 vol., edited by Pablo Pastells, Barcelona, 1900-1902.

Conklin, Harold C. "Betel Chewing among the Hanunoo." Abstract No. 66, *Fourth Far-Eastern Prehistory Congress.* Special reprint. Diliman, Quezon City: National Research Council of the Philippines, U.P., 1958.

———. "Betel Chewing among the Hanunoo." *Philippine Heritage: The Making of a Nation.* Sydney: Hamlyn House, 1974.

———. *Hanunoo Agriculture, A Report on an Integral System of Shifting Cultivation in the Philippines.* Rome: Food and Agriculture Organization of the United Nations, 1957.

———. *Hanunoo-English Vocabulary.* Berkeley: University of California Press, 1953.

———. "Maling, A Hanunoo Girl from the Philippines." *In the Company of Man.* New York: Harper and Harper, 1960.

De la Costa, H., S.J. *The Jesuits in the Philippines, 1581-1768.* Cambridge, Mass.: Harvard University Press, 1961.

———. *Readings in Philippine History.* Manila: 1965, 1973.

Echevarria, Ramon. *Rediscovery in Southern Cebu.* Cebu City: Barba Press, 1974.

Gardner, Fletcher. *Indic Writings of the Mindoro-Palawan Axis.* San Antonio, Texas: Witte Memorial Museum, 1940.

———. *Philippine Indic Studies.* San Antonio, Texas: The Witte Memorial Museum, 1943.

Hartendorp, A. V. H. *The Japanese Occupation of the Philippines.* Vol. 2. Manila: Bookmark, 1967.

Jagor, Fedor. *Travels in the Philippines.* London: Chapman and Hall, 1875.

Jordana y Morera, Ramon. *Memoria Sobre la Producción de los Montes Publicos de Filipinas en el Año Economico de 1871-72. Elevada el Excmo, Sr. Ministro de Ultramar.* Madrid, M. Minuesa, 1874.

──────────. *Bosquejo Geografica e Historico Natural del Archipelago Filipino.* Madrid: Impr. de Moreno y Roxas, 1885.

──────────. *Estudio Forestal Acerca de la India Inglesa, Java y Filipinas.* Madrid: Moreno y Roxas, 1891.

Keesing, Felix M. *The Ethnohistory of Northern Luzon.* Stanford, California: Stanford University Press, 1962.

Landicho, Macario Z. *Mindoro Yearbook, 1901-1951.* Manila: Yearbook Publishers, 1952.

Landor, Henry Savage. *The Gems of the East.* New York: Harper and Brothers, 1904.

Le Gentil de la Galaisiére. *A Voyage Round the World.* Manila: Filipiniana Book Guild, 1964.

Lopez, Juan. "Events in the Filipinas." In E. H. Blair and J. A. Robertson, Vol. 27, p. 36.

Lopez, Rafael et al. *The Christianization of the Philippines.* Manila: 1965.

Majul, Cesar A. *Muslims in the Philippines.* Quezon City: University of the Philippines Press, 1973.

Maldonaldo, Juan Pacheco. "Letter to Felipe II," Manila (1575?). In E. H. Blair and J. A. Robertson, Vol. 3, p. 299.

Manuscrito inedito, "Relacion de la conquista de la Isla de Luzon," fechado en Manila, el 20 de Abril de 1972. In Wenceslao E. Retana *Archivo del Bibliofico Filipino.* Madrid, 1898, p. 4.

Marche, Alfredo. *Luzon and Palawan.* Translated from the French by Carmen Ojeda and Jovita Castro. Manila: The Filipiniana Book Guild, 1970.

Medina, Juan de. "History of the Agustinian Order in the Filipinas Islands," 1630 but printed in Manila, 1898. In E. H. Blair and J. A. Robertson, Vol. 22, p. 222.

Meyer, Adolf Bernhard. *Die Mangianenschrift von Mindoro.* hrsg. von A. B. Meyer and A. Schadenberg. Special bearb. von W. Foy, R. Friedlander, 1895.

Mirandaola, Andres de. "Letter to Felipe II." Cebu, June 8, 1569. In E. H. Blair and J. A. Robertson, Vol. 3, p. 38.

Montano, Joseph. Rapport a monsieur de Ministre de l' Instruccion

Publique sur une Mission aux Iles Philippines et en Malaise (1879-1881). Paris, Imprimerie Nationale, 1885.

———————. *Voyage aux Philippines et en Malaisie.* Paris: Hachette, 1886.

Montero y Vidal, D. Jose. *Historia de la Pirateria Malayo-mahometana en Mindanao.* Tomo I. Madrid: Imprenta y Fundacion de Manuel Tellos, 1888.

Morga, Antonio de. *Sucesos de las Islas Filipinas.* Translated by Encarnacion Alzona and annotated by Jose Rizal. Manila: Jose Rizal National Centennial Commission, 1962.

Navarrete, Domingo, O.P. 1676. "Manila and the Philippines About 1650" (concluded) in E. H. Blair and J. A. Robertson, Vol. 38, 1674-1683.

Ortega, Francisco de. "Report Concerning Filipinas Islands and Other Papers." In E. H. Blair and J. A. Robertson, Vol. 9, p. 98.

Schebesta, Paul. *Menschen Ohne Ceschichte.* Modling, Verlag-der Missionsdruchere St. Gabriel, 1947.

Scott, William Henry. *Prehispanic Source Materials for the Study of Philippine History.* Manila: University of Santo Tomas Press, 1968.

——————— and Ju I-hsiung. Chau Ju-Kua's description of the Philippines in the 13th Century: a new translation of *Historical Bulletin,* Vol. 2, No. 1 (March, 1967), pp. 69-72.

Sharp, Andrew. *Adventurous Armada, The Story of Legaspi's Expedition.* Christchurch, New Zealand: Whitcombe and Tombs, Ltd., 1961.

Stickley, Caroline. *Broken Snare.* London: OMF Books, 1975.

Velarde, Pedro Murillo, S.J. *Historia de la Provincia de Philippinas de la Compania de Jesus.* Segundo parte, qve, comprehende los progresos de esta provincia desde el año de 1616 hasta el año de 1716. Manila: Imprenta de la Compania de Jesus por de Nicolas de la Cruz Bagay, 1749, (13), 419, (6) leaves, map.

Worcester, Dean C. *The Philippine Islands and Their People.* New York: The Macmillan Co., 1899.

———————. *The Philippines, Past and Present.* New York: The Macmillan Co., 1930.

Zuñiga, Joaquin Martinez de. *Status of the Philippines in 1800.* Translated from Spanish by Vicente del Carmen. Manila: Filipiniana Book Guild, 1973.

Government Publications

Annual Reports of the War Department. Vol. 10, Part I. Washington: Government Printing Office, 1905.

Annual Reports of the War Department. Vol. 11, Part I. Washington: Government Printing Office, 1905.

Annual Reports of the War Department. Vol. 11, Part II. Washington: Government Printing Office, 1905.

Annual Reports of the War Department. 1905, Vol. 13, Part III. Washington: Government Printing Office, 1906.

Barrows, David P. "History of the Population." *Census of the Philippine Islands.* Vol. 1. Washington: U.S. Bureau of the Census, 1905, p. 547.

Census of the Philippine Islands: 1903. 4 vols., 2nd ed. Washington: United States Bureau of the Census, 1905.

Census of the Philippine Island: 1918. 4 vols. Manila: Census of the Philippine Islands, 1921.

Commission on National Integration Report. 1973. Quezon City: CNI Office, 1973.

Third Annual Report of the Philippine Commission: 1902. Part I. Washington: Government Printing Office, 1903.

Fourth Annual Report of the Philippine Commission: 1903. Part II. Washington: Government Printing Office, 1904.

Fifth Annual Report of the Philippine Commission: 1904. Part II. Washington: Government Printing Office, 1905.

Messages of the President. Vol. 2, Part I. Revised Ed. Manila: Bureau of Printing, 1938.

Messages of the President. Vol. 4, Part II. Manila: Bureau of Printing, 1939.

Philippine Reports. Vol. 22. Manila: Bureau of Printing, 1918.

Report of the Philippine Commission to the Secretary of War: 1909-1911. Washington: Government Printing Office, n.d.

Report of the Philippine Commission to the Secretary of War: 1913. Washington: Government Printing Office, 1914.

Report of the Philippine Commission to the Secretary of War: July 1, 1913–Dec. 31, 1914. Washington: Government Printing Office, 1915.

Report of the Governor-General of the Philippine Islands to the Secretary of War: 1916. Washington: Government Printing Office, 1917.

Report of the Governor-General of the Philippine Islands to the Secretary of War. Washington: Government Printing Office, 1918.
Report of the Governor-General of the Philippine Islands to the Secretary of War: 1924. Washington: Government Printing Office, 1925.
Report of the Governor-General of the Philippine Islands to the Secretary of War. Washington: Government Printing Office, 1926.
Republic of the Philippines Manual. Office of Public Information, Malacañang, Manila: Bureau of Printing, 1930.
Revised Administrative Code of the Philippine Islands. 1934. Supplementary Materials. Washington: Government Printing Office, 1945.
Reyes, Alice H. and Rodriguez, Artemio S., eds. *Journal of National Integration.* Quezon City: Commission on National Integration, 1968.

PERIODICAL ARTICLES

Anonymous. "The Island of Mindoro." *The Journal of Indian Archipelago and Eastern Asia.* Singapore: Series I, Vol. 3, 1849.
Barham, Marie. "The Phonemes of the Buhid (Mangyan) Language of Eastern Mindoro." *Oceania Linguistic Monographs* 3: 4-9. Capell and Wurms, eds. (1955).
Bartlett, Harley Harris. "The geographic distribution, migration and dialectal mutation of certain plant names in the Philippines and Netherlands Indies with special references to the materia medica of a Mangyan mediquillo." *Proceedings of the Sixth Pacific Science Congress,* Vol. 4, Berkeley, 1934, pp. 85-109.
──────. "The geographic distribution, migration and dialectal mutation of certain plant names in the Philippines and Netherlands India with special reference to the materials medica of a Mangyan mediquillo." *Proceedings of the Sixth Pacific Science Congress of the Pacific Science Association.* Berkeley and Los Angeles, 6(4): 85-110 (1940).
Blumentritt, Ferdinand. "Die Mangianenschrift von Mindoro." *Globus* Vol. 69, No. II (March 1896), 163-66.
──────. "Die Manguianen der Insel Mindoro (Philippinen)." *Globus,* Vol. 50.
Cinco, Meren Nata. "The White Race of Mindoro." *Philippine Maga-*

zine, Vol. 23, No. 7 (December 1926), pp. 393-94.
Conklin, Harold C. "Buhid Pottery." *University of Manila Journal of East Asiatic Studies,* Vol. 3, No. 1.
───────. "Preliminary Report on Field Work on the Islands of Mindoro and Palawan." *American Anthropologist,* II, 2 (April-June 1949).
Ganzon, G. Fores. "A critical study of some investigations made of our Pre-Historic Past." *Philippine Social Sciences and Humanities Review,* Vol. 17 (March 1952), p. 3.
Gardner, Fletcher. "Three contemporary incised bamboo manuscripts from Hampangan Mangyan, Mindoro, Philippine Islands." *Journal of the American Oriental Society* 59(4): 496-502, (1939).
───────. "Lingualization in Austronesian Languages: An Unusual Consonantal Shift." *Papers of the Michigan Academy of Science, Arts and Letters,* Vol. 27, pp. 511-14. Ann Arbor: University of Michigan Press.
Lopez, Violeta B. "Culture Contact and Ethnogenesis in Mindoro Up to the End of the Spanish Rule." A reprint from *Asian Studies,* Vol. 12, No. 1 (April 1974), pp. 1-38.
───────. "Towards Integration—A Review of Policies Affecting the Minority Groups with Special Reference to the Mangyans (1901-1975)." A reprint from *Asian Studies,* Vol. 12, Nos. 2 and 3 (August-December 1974), pp. 86-99.
MacDonald, Charles. "Notes de Terrain: Mindoro Philippines." *Lanques Et Techniques Nature Et Societe.* Edite par Jacqueline M.C. Thomas and Lucien Benot, Editions Klincksieck, (1971).
MacDonald, Nicole Revel. "La Collecte Du Miel." *Langues Et Techniques Nature Et Societe,* Editions Klincksieck, (1971).
Maceda, Marcelino N. "A Brief Report on some Mangyans Northern Oriental Mindoro." *Unitas* 40(1): 102-55, (1967).
Muratake, Seiichi and Yasushi Kikuchi. "Social Structure of the Batangan in Mindoro, Philippines." *SHA, A Quarterly Record of Social Anthropology,* Vol. 11, No. 2 (October 1968), pp. 30-61.
Postma, Antoon. "Development Among the Mangyans." *Philippine Quarterly of Culture and Society,* Vol. 12, Nos. 1-2. Offprint copy.
Rivera y Olarte, C. I. "The Country of Ma-i: An Old Chinese Account of the Philippines in the 13th Century." *Sunday Times Magazine,* July 8, 1962, pp. 14-15.

Schneider, Edwin Emil. "Notes on the Mangyan Language." *Philippine Journal of Science* 7(3, Section D): 157-58. (1912).

Wang Teh-Ming. "Sino-Filipino historico-cultural relations." *Philippine Social Sciences and Humanities Review,* Vol. 29, No. 3-4 (September-December 1964).

UNPUBLISHED MATERIALS

Almero, Felix. "Customs and Mores of the Mangyans of Occidental Mindoro." Unpublished master's thesis, Far Eastern University, 1951.

Bobon, Fe A. "The Hanunoo Mangyan in Panaytayan, Mansalay, Oriental Mindoro." Unpublished master's thesis, University of Manila, 1970.

Calleja, Marcelino. "A Study of the Culture of the Mangyans of Mindoro." Unpublished master's thesis, Lyceum of the Philippines, Manila, 1960.

Conklin, Harold C. "The Relation of Hanunoo Culture to the Plant World." Unpublished Ph.D. dissertation, Yale University.

Dimalibot, P. E. "Life and Culture of the Mangyans of Occidental Mindoro." Unpublished master's thesis, National University, 1955.

Estel, Leon Arthur. "Mindoro Anthropometry and Racial Origins in Northern Indonesia." Berkeley: University of California, 1950.

Gardner, Fletcher. "Letters Relating to the Mangyans of Mindoro." (1904). Manuscript bound in Mindoro-Palawan Papers, Beyer Collection: Philippine Ethnography—A collection of original sources. Cambridge: Harvard University microreproduction.

——————. "The Mangyans." Manuscript bound in Mindoro-Palawan Papers, Beyer Collection: Philippine Ethnography—A collection of original sources.

——————. "The Hampangan Mangyans of Mindoro." Beyer Collection.

Iturralde, Encarnacion. "The Religion of the Mangyans of Mindoro: An Anthropological Approach to Mission Work." Ph.D. dissertation, University of Sto. Tomas Graduate School, Manila: June 1973.

Johnston, May. "Mindoro's Gold." (May 1974).

Leeder, Leo L. "A Survey of Pagan Tribes in the Philippines and of Missionary Efforts Toward Their Evangelization." Unpublished master's thesis. Columbia Bible College Graduate School of Missions. (May, 1956).

Leviste, Mercedes A. "The Role of the Saclag Settlement Schools in the Uplift of the Lives of the Mangyans." Unpublished master's thesis, University of Sto. Tomas, 1964.

Paz, Emeterio de la, S.V.D. "A Survey of the Hanunoo Mangyan Culture." Unpublished master's thesis, University of Santo Tomas, 1967.

Tolentino, Mila S. "Some Aspects of Iraya Mangyan Culture and Their Implications for Education Programming." Unpublished master's thesis, University of the East, 1969.

Tweddell, Colin E. "The Iraya (Mangyan) Language of Mindoro, Philippines: Phonology and Morphology." Unpublished Ph.D. dissertation. University of Washington.

Index

Abra de Ilog, 40
Act No. 1396, Sept. 4, 1905; 110 see also "Special Provincial Government Act"
Admixture
  Concept of, 125
  Encouragement of, 108
Adultery, 52
Los Aetas, 49
Agoncillo, Teodoro A., 33, 35
Agusan, 115
Alabes, Diego, 37
Alangan Mangyan, 58, 66, 100
Albuquerque, de, Fray, 24
Alcalde mayor, 33, 35
  Abuses of, 35
Ambahan, 44, 103, 128
  Poetry, 63
American civil government
  Policies toward the minority groups
  Re-examination of, 112
American colonial rule, 126
American colonizers, 98
American enterprise
  Pressures from, 84-89
American Ethnology
  Bureau of, 109
Americans
  "Protector of the Mangyans", 85
Augustinian missionaries, 26
Aves de Rapiña case, 85

Baclayan, Puerto Galera, 6
Baco Mangyan, 61

Baco river, 19, 22, 60
Baco village, 26
Ba-iac, 12
Balatamay, 39
Bandits see Tulisanes
Bangon Mangyan, 64, 66, 100
"Banguu", 43-44
Banton island, 19
Barangay, 127
Barham, Marie, 100
Barrantes, Vicente, 36
Barrio officials
  Election of, 104
Barrows, David, 107-09
  Proposals made by, 108
  Report of, 107-08
Batangan Mangyan, 3, 66, 73, 100
  Legend of, 3
Batangas, 42-43
  Separation of Mindoro from, 33
Bayanan, Puerto Galera, 6
"Benevolence", 85
Beyer, H. Otley, 4, 5-6
Bicol Region, 32
Bisayan culture, 124
Blood-brotherhood, 89-90 see also Sanduguan, Rite of
Blumentritt, Ferdinand, 11, 48, 49-50, 124
Bongabong, Mindoro, 62
Bornean preacher-traders, 24
Buisan, Datu, 37
Buhid Mangyan, 44, 58, 100, 126, 128

145

Literature of, 44
Marriage practice of, 101
Bukid Mangyan, 63, 64, 66
Bukidnon, 115
Bulalacao, Mindoro, 41, 90
Buquiles, 8-9, 47, 48
Bureau of American Ethnology *see* American Ethnology, Bureau of
Bureau of Non-Christian Tribes *see* Non-Christian Tribes, Bureau of

CNI *see* National Integration, Commission on
Calamianes, 37
Calavite Point, 40
Calilaya, 36
Camucones, 30
Careri, Gemelli, 3
Catholic Church
 Spiritual accomplishments of, 98
Catholic faith, 22, 98, 123
 Rekindling of, 30
Catholic schools
 Establishment of, 98
Cebu
 Portuguese forces in, 14
Celadon wares, 5
Chao, Ju-Kua, 7, 10, 11-12
"Chichimecos", 7, 8, 19, 24, 28 *see also* Negritoes
China Inland Mission
 Report, 99-100
Chinese merchants, 14, 23
Chinese porcelain, 7
Chinese potteries, 5
Chinese settlements, 14
Chinese state documents, 7
Chinese traders, 7, 10, 22
Christ of Burgos, 31-32
"Christian landgrabbers", 116
Christian lowlanders, 9
 Pressures from, 89-98
Christian settlements
 Piratical assaults in, 8
Christianization, 8
Chu-Fan-Chi, 10
Church and State
 Separation of, 98
Class consciousness, 87
Clavel, Leothiny, 109
Coastal people, 19, 23
 Description, 23-24
Colin, Francisco, 25, 29, 33-35
Colonial pressure
 Response to, 122
Commisario de Manguianes, 51

Commission on National Integration *see* National Integration, Commission on
Common nationality, 114
Congressional committee
 Achievements of, 118
 Findings of, 117-18
Conklin, Harold C., 58, 65-66, 97, 117
"Conquistadores" see Spanish colonizers
Corregidor, 33
Corregimiento, 33
Cotabato, 115
Cross and the Sword
 Symbols of, 122
Cross-ethnic communication, 128
"Cross-ethnic" relations, 124
"Cultural communities", 126
Cultural identity, 120
"Cultural minorities", 126
Culture
 Hispanized, 9
Culture lag, 97
Cultures
 Differentiation of, 123
 Diversification of, 21-22
Cuyonon, 58

Damuong, 91
Davao, 115
David, Jesse D., 114
Dennison, Winfred T., 114

Echevaria, Ramon, 122
Elim island, 16
Encomendero, 33
Encomienda, 32-33
 Theory, 33
Encomiendas de particulares, 33
Entradas, 32
Estel, Leo, 67, 69-70
Ethnological Survey of the Philippines, 64, 87, 109
Evangelista, Alfredo, 4
Evangelization
 Repercussions from, 98-105
Excavations
 Philippine, 6
Exploitation
 Chain of, 85
Extinction
 Threat of, 126

Fidelity
 Christian concept of, 101
Filipino culture
 Unification of, 128

INDEX

Filipino national heritage, 128
Friar missionary, 33

Gardner, Fletcher, 6, 11, 41, 58, 61-62, 85, 86-87, 89, 92, 96
German anthropologist, 111
German Catholic mission, 98
Gihitän, 63
God
   Monotheistic concept of, 52
Goiti, Martin de, 18, 20, 22, 23, 28
Gold, 14
Gomez, Jose, 39
Grave sites
   In Puerto Galera, 6
Greater East Asia Co-Prosperity Sphere, 94
Guerras piraticas de Filipinas, 36
Gutierrez, Pedro, 39
Guzman, Enriquez de, 32

Habeas corpus law, 116
Hampangan Mangyan, 62
   Exploitation of, 89
   Syllabary, 63
Hanono-o Mangyan *see* Hanunoo Mangyan
Hanunoo Mangyan, 44, 48, 58, 62, 66, 67, 100, 103, 104, 117, 128
   Education of, 103
   Isolationist attitude of, 97
   Life, 66
   Response to pressures of, 97
   Socio-political structure of
      Change in, 104
   System of beliefs of, 99
Hispanization, 123
   Pattern of, 8
   Process of, 25
Hispanized culture, 9
Hispanized lowlanders *see* Christian lowlanders
Historia de la pirateria, 36

Ilin, 32, 40
I-Ling, 13
Imitation
   As a response, 87
Indian society, 109
Infieles, 106, 123
"Integration"
   Concept of, 57-58, 116, 124-26
   Policy of, 58-59
   Problem of, 9
Intermarriage, 8, 30
Inter-tribal fellowship of believers
   Establishment of, 102

Interior
   Department of, 114, 117
Iraya-Alangan Mangyan, 60, 72
Iraya Mangyan, 58, 66, 67, 100, 119, 128
Iron-Age site in Mindoro, 5
Islam, 24
Islamic area force in the South, 8
Isolation, 125
   Policy of, 57, 58, 98, 108
Isolationist attitude, 97
Iturralde, 58, 70

Japanese rule, 94
Jesuit missionaries, 27, 29
Jimenez, Alonzo, 32
Johnston, May, 102
Jordana, Ramon Morera, 41, 47, 48, 50-52, 124

Kaig, 112
Kalaw, Teodoro M., 85
Ka-Ma-Yan, 13-14
Ka-Mangyan, 14
Keesing, Felix M., 45
Kikuchi, Yasushi, 58, 72, 73

La Galaisiere, Le Gentil de, 3
Lalauigan, 111
Lanao, 115
Land-grabbing, 93-94, 96
Landicho, Macario Z., 98, 117
Landor, A. Henry Savage, 61
Leadership
   Modern form of, 104
Legaspi, 14
Leo XIII, *Pope,* 98
Lewis and Clark exposition, 86
Lillo, Maximo, 50
Limahong, 26
Lipa
   Diocese of, 98
Locsin, Cecilia, 6
Locsin, Leandro, 6
Lopez, Juan, 37
Lowland exploitation, 44
Lubang island, 18, 32
Luzon
   Conquest of, 19

MacDonald, Charles, 58, 72
Maceda, Marcelino, 67, 69
Maguindanao fleet, 37
Ma-i, 10-11, 14
   Description, 11-12
Mait, 11
   Meaning, 11

Majority-minority relations
  Worcester's view of, 113
Majul, Cesar, 36, 37
Malaguia, 53
Malay immigrants, 8
"Malayan society", 109
Maldonado, Juan Pacheco, 25
Mamburau, 16
"Mangians", 27
"Manguianes", 44, 48, 84
Mangyan Bible School, 102-03, 128
  Establishment of, 102
  Policy of, 102
  Use of Pilipino in, 128
Mangyan Church
  Conferences, 102
Mangyan civil rights, 115
"Mangyan-Christian dichotomy", 25
Mangyan cultures
  Preservation of, 127
  Unification of, 128
Mangyan development program, 112
Mangyan idioms, 50
Manyan inter-"tribal" conferences, 128
  Use of Pilipino in, 128
Mangyan leaders
  Biblical training for, 102
Mangyan life
  Pressures on, 59, 123
  New, 126
Mangyan-lowland Christian dichotomy, 7-8, 123
Mangyan mediquillo, 65
Mang-Yan San, 13
Mangyan script, 49-50
Mangyan woman
  Conversion of, 30
Mangyans, 8
  Catholic missions among, 29
  And Christian lowlanders
    Social distance between, 9
  Classification of, 47-48, 64, 65
  Conversion of, 105
  Description, 27-28, 30
  Ethnographic groups of, 66
  Legal customs of, 52
  Morals and ethics of, 52
  Popular myth about, 3
  Religious pressure on
    Weakening of, 98
  Sub-human treatment of, 91
Manila, 40
  Limahong's attack on, 26
  Spanish settlements in, 19
Mansalay, Oriental Mindoro, 103
Marinduque, 27, 39, 110
Maritime courtesy
  Breach of, 23

Marriage, 53
Masbate
  Spanish sovereignty in, 32
Mauhaw river, 11
Mayit, 11
Medina, Juan de, 26, 27
Meyer, Adolf Bernhard, 49-50
Miller, Merton, 64, 87, 89, 107, 109
Mindanao, 39, 115, 117
Mindanao and Sulu
  Department of
    Abolition of, 115
Mindoro
  Chinese traders in, 22-24
  As a commercial port, 23
  Creation as an apostolic-prefecture, 98
  Description, 19
  Detachment from Marinduque province, 110
  Epidemic in 1902; 83
  Governor
    Authorization given to, 110
    Roles of, 110
  Japanese occupation of, 117
  Land problems in, 116
  Missionary activity in
    Reduction of, 98
  Muslim piratical activity in, 123-24
  Native inhabitants of
    Origin, 4
  Pre-Spanish, 10-14
  Religious impact in
    Weakening of, 98
  Spanish period, 14-22
Mindoro Sugar Company, 85
Ming celadons, 6
Ming dynasty, 7, 13
Minolo, Puerto Galera, 6, 11
Minority
  Concept of, 57, 125
"Minority group", 9
Min-to-lang, 12, 14
  Description, 12-13
Min-To-Long *see* Min-to-lang
Missionary activity
  Revival of, 29
Missionary ethics and beliefs, 101
Mojica, Diego, 26
Monogamy
  Christian concept of, 101
Montano, Joseph, 41, 42
Montero, Jose Vidal, 35, 36, 39, 40
Morga, Antonio A., 35-36, 42
"Moro attacks", 41
"Moro bandits", 117
"Moro country", 114
"Moro pirates", 41
"Moro" piratical operations, 123

INDEX

Moro wars, 36
"Moros", 19, 20, 24, 65, 106
Mt. Halcon, 72, 94, 117
Mt. Province, 114, 115
Municipal government in Mindoro, 110
Muslim attacks, 37
Muslim Bornean settlers, 24
Muslim-Christian relations, 117
Muslim piracy, 41, 123
    Effect of, 124
    Rise of, 36
Muslim pirates, 9, 39, 43
Muslims, 115
    Integration, 117
Muslims in the Philippines, 36
"Mutual distrust and hatred", 113

National Assembly
    First, 116
National community
    Concept of, 124
National Cultural Minorities, 118
National Integration, 120, 126-27
    Commission on, 118, 119
        Creation of, 118
        Functions, 118-19
        See also R.A. 1888
National Museum *see* Philippine National Museum
National Resettlement and Rehabilitation Administration, 118
Nationality
    Concept of, 59
Nauhan Mangyan, 66, 67
Nauhan-Pola Mangyan, 100
Naujan, Mindoro, 27, 30
Navarrete, Domingo, 29, 30
Negritoes, 8 *see also* "Chichemecos"
New Spain, 23
New Tribes Mission, 100
"Non-Christian" tribes, 57, 125
    Bureau of, 109, 116
        Abolition of
            Significance of, 116
        Creation of, 107
        Duties, 114-15
        Objectives, 107
        Reconstitution of, 114
Nueva Vizcaya, 115

O.M.F. *see* Overseas Missionary Fellowship
Offley, Robert G., 83, 92-93, 111
Olarte, 11
Ordoñez, Niurio, 90
Ortega, Francisco de, 26

Overseas Missionary Fellowship, 100, 128
    Achievements of, 102

Pacific War, 1941; 117
Page, Hazel, 100
Palaeolithic Age, 4
Panay, 14, 18
Paterno, Pedro A., 49, 50
Pautangan system, 51
Peace
    Treaty for, 20
"Peace and order" in the South, 117
Peñalver, Domingo de, 27
Pennoyer, Douglas, 58, 73
Philip II, *King*, 25
Philippine Bill of 1913; 113
Philippine Church
    Reorganization of, 98
Philippine Commission, 93, 108, 110, 114
    Annual report to, 113
    Report of, 87
Philippine excavations
    History, 6
Philippine Iron Age, 5
Philippine Legislature, 85
Philippine National Museum, 4, 6
Philippines
    Colonization of, 7
    History
        New era in, 116
Pilipino language
    As a medium of communication, 128
"Pillaging business", 39
Pinamalayan, Oriental Mindoro, 40
"Pintados", 23
Piracy, 8, 36
    Spread of, 9
Pirates, 9 *see also* Muslim pirates
Poale, Eduard L., 84
Policy of isolation, 57
Political subjugation, 33
Population
    Backward elements of, 114
Porcelain Age, 4
    Culture, 5
Portugal, 14
Portuguese forces in Cebu, 14
Postma, Antoon, 58, 71, 97, 98, 103, 104-05
    Missionary work of, 103, 104
Power
    Abuse of, 35
    Concentration of, 35
"Presidente", 111
Pressures
    Responses of Mangyans to, 96

Primitive justice
 Act of, 96
Property
 Individual ownership of, 108
Protestant missionaries
 Report of, 94-95
Puerto Galera, 33
 Excavations made in, 6
"Punta de Sto. Tomas", 40

Qudarat, Sultan, 37
Quezon, Manuel Luis, 116

R.A. 1888; 118 see also National Integration, Commission on
Rada, Martin de, 33
Rancheria, 51
Ratagnon Mangyan, 58, 64, 66, 100
Reducciones, 27
Reform decrees
 Of 1844; 35
 Of 1886; 35
Religious activity
 Lull in, 29
Religious evangelization, 25, 123
 Lag in, 27
Religious revival
 Consequences of, 31-32
Religious strain, 123
Reports on the South Seas barbarians, 10
Reservation system, 108
Retana, 33
Revolution of 1896; 114
Rizal, Jose A., 12, 42
"Ruby vs. the Provincial Board of Mindoro", 107

St. Louis exposition, 57
Salcedo, Juan de, 14, 16, 18, 32, 39
 Expedition of, 14, 16
Samahan ng mga Pantribong Iglesiyang Ebanhelika ng Mangyan, 102
Samahang Nayon, 127
Samar, 40
San Antonio, Juan Francisco de, 11
San Jose sugar estate, 84
San Vitores, Diego Luis de, 29
Sanduguan
 Rite of, 89-90 see also Blood-brotherhood
Sangleyes, 22
Santos, Lope K., 85
Saucedo, Philippe de, 33
"Savage" ethnic groups, 57
Sawankhalok potteries, 6
Schadenberg, A., 49, 50

Schebesta, Paul, 58, 65, 69, 111-12
Scott, William Henry, 11
Scripture
 Translation into Mangyan dialects, 100
Self-government, 113
Settlement system
 Failure of, 111
"Sexual escapade", 91
Sheriff force
 Use of, 88, 111
A short account of the islands barbarians, 12
Sino-Philippine cultural relations, 10
Slavery, 51
Social dysphoria, 120
Social Welfare Administration, 119
Society of the Divine Word, 98
Socol, Mindoro, 41
Solheim, Wilhelm G., 5
Southeast Asian nationalities, 23
Spaniards, 122
 Abuses of, 42
 Coming of, 14
 Peaceful attitude of, 20
 Pressures from
  Response of the natives to, 16
Spanish colonial expansion, 122
Spanish colonial power, 8
Spanish colonial rule
 Effects of, 32-36
 Muslim response to, 123
Spanish colonizers, 7-8
Spanish control
 Oppressive system of, 51
 Sphere of, 122-123
Spanish cultural practices, 123
Spanish expedition, 32
Spanish forces
 And Moros of Mindoro
  Encounter between, 20
 Strength of, 21
Spanish governor-general, 14
Spanish historians, 23
Spanish missionaries
 Religious influence of, 32, 123
Spanish-Muslim conflict, 8
Spanish pressure
 Creative response to, 21
Spanish settlements
 In Manila, 19
 In Mindoro, 19
"Spanish sword", 16
"Special provinces", 110, 115
 Organization and administration of, 110
"Special Provincial Government Act", 110
"Splendid isolation", 97

INDEX

Status quo
   Defense of, 112
Stickley, Carolyn, 95-96
The Study on the Eastern and Western Oceans, 13
Sulu, 115, 117
Sung celadons, 6
Sun dynasty, 7
Supreme Court decision, 88, 107

Tadyawan Mangyan, 58, 95, 96
Tagal Mangyan, 27, 37, 39
Taga-gaba Mangyan, 69
Taga-langan Mangyan, 69
Tagalog, 47
   As a medium of instruction, 102
Tagalog culture, 127, 128
"Tagalog Filipinos"
   Attitude of, 111
Taga-ulunan Mangyan, 69
"Tailed-people" of Mindoro, 3
Tamano, Mamintal, 109
Tamaraw, 13
Tangalan, Puerto Galera, 6
Tao-i-Chih (A Short Account of the Islands Barbarians), 12
Tawbuid Mangyan, 58, 72-73
Territorial rights, 8
Tidunes *see* Tirones
Tirones, 9
Total society, 9
"Treaty for peace", 20
Tribal research, 115
Tribute, 33
   Collection of, 33, 35

Tulin, Mindoro, 41
Tulisanes, 83
Tung-Si-Yang-Kao (The Study on the Eastern and Western Oceans), 13
Tweddel, Colin E., 58, 70

Urukay, 44

"Vaco, Mindoro", 33
Valencia, Ramon, 50
Varadero, 36
Velarde, Pedro Murillo, 28-29, 30-32

Wang, Ta-Yuan, 7, 12
Wang, Teh-Ming, 12, 13
Welch and Fairchild and Co., 84, 85
"White race" of Mindoro, 3
Williamson, Frances, 100
"Withdrawal", 96
   Response of, 123, 124
Worcester, Dean C., 58, 60, 83, 84, 85, 86,, 93-110, 111, 112-13
   Ethnographic research made by, 60-61
   Report of, 112, 114

Yuan dynasty, 12

Zaitun port, 12
Zamboanga, 115
Zibuyan island, 19
Zuñiga, Joaquin de, 40
Zuñiga, Martinez de, 37